Anne of Green Gables
the Musical
101 Things you didn't know

Anne of Green Gables
the Musical

101 Things you didn't know

Don Harron

Dedicated with much love to my two best friends
Norman & Elaine Campbell

White Knight Books

National Library of Canada Cataloguing in Publication Data

Harron, Don, 1924-
    Anne of Green Gables, the musical : 101 things you didn't know / Don Harron. — First ed.

Includes index.
ISBN 978-1-897456-03-3

1. Campbell, Norman, 1924- Anne of Green Gables.
2. Musicals — Canada — History and criticism.   I. Title.

ML410.C189H32 2008   782.14   C2008-901174-0

Published in 2008 by
White Knight Books, a division of Bill Belfontaine Ltd.
Suite 304, 160 Balmoral Avenue, Toronto Ontario Canada M4V 1J7
T. 416-925-6458 F. 416-925-4165 e-mail whitekn@istar.ca
distributed by White Knight Book Distribution Services Ltd.
Web site: www.whiteknightbookdistributionservices.com

1 2 3 4 5 – 12 11 10 09 08

Design: Fortunato Design Inc.
Printed and bound in Canada

Acknowledgments

Instead of listing all the people who helped me bring forth this book I'd like to go into more detail about their contributions. First of all there is my White Knight Book publisher, Bill Belfontaine, who dragged me away from a fourteen year hiatus and talked me into writing another Charlie Farquharson tome called year "Fifty Years of Farquharson Around."

Then there is his buddy Bill Hushion, who shepherded me through many Charlie books from "Histry of Canada" to "Olde Charlie Farquharson's Testament."

I also have the good fortune of being reunited with my friend who did all the art work in those books, Fortunato Aglialoro, took this picture for the cover and made me look "adoptable." I am forever grateful.

However Bill H. told Bill B. to hold off on the Farquharson book, because 2008 is the year of the centennial of Lucy Maud Montgomery's great classic You-know-who of Green Gables. Bill Hushion suggested that, for a change, I should write a book in English, instead of my usual broken Canadian-Parry-Sound-patois. Being the last surviving member of the creative team of the musical version of the novel, I agreed, and Bill H. suggested that I should call the book "*A Hundred Things You Didn't Know About Anne of Green Gables, the Musical*". The fact that it turned out to be "*One Hundred And One Things, etc*", oh well…what can I say, there was so much good material.

I could not have begun this project without the help of my lady love, Claudette. I had to reach friends far and wide and let them know that I needed their help and their input. Claudette did that, and more. She has seen many presentations of this musical with me, but somehow she still cries during the overture. As the editor of this book, she is the true spirit of this enterprise.

A thing I had to do on my own, was travel to Charlottetown, long after the season had closed. I checked in with the Charlottetown Festival for help. Brenda Gallant and Cindy Riley were more than ready to help me. They got me appointments with the chiefs of the backstage crew, Roddy Diamond and Rich Wilson who still seem enthusiastic about doing the show after more than forty years. They have seen 3149 Annes, and gave me backstage stories that stretched all the way to New York and Japan.

Then Paul Smitz came into lunch from his island rural retreat and gave me the cool whip story plus other backstage legends.

David Mackenzie, the head hauncho CEO, gave me a scurrilous onstage story and made me promise I wouldn't give him credit. Done, David.

Hank Stinson, Charlottetown Festival's utility man, was busy with his revival of Lucy Maud's "Blue Castle" but promised to send me stuff, and did. Thanks Hank.

Jack McAndrew and his wife Barbara came in from Meadowbank to chew over those first formative years. Thanks.

I finally tracked down that perpetual performer, perky Glenda Landry. She took time off from her chef's duties at Sim's elegant restaurant one morning to regale me with great stories about her 38 year career with the Festival. (She sure don't look it!) She said I had just missed Gracie Finley, who has a place on the Island, but luckily I reached her at her English home and got great stuff. Gracie and Glenda are still bosom friends and kindred spirits, and so are Toby Tarnow and Nonnie Griffin, TV's original Anne and Diana. Thanks to all four for precious lore.

A special thank you to multi-time Anne performer Leisa Way who gave me a hilarious story about the department store tour of Japan in '89 that led to the full-cast Japanese tour in 1991. For details of that tour I am forever grateful to Denise Fergusson who loaned me copies of her columns written for the event in her home-town paper the St. Mary's Journal-Argus, as well as her own personal observations both before and after that monumental tour plus the fun things that happened backstage in 1994. I promise I will return everything later.

A special thank you to everyone who loaned me their precious pictures, I will return them, I promise, unlike a certain Charlie Farquharson who never does….

Thanks to: Doug Adler, Annie Allan, Angie Antonelli, Malcolm Black, Howard Cable, Justine Campbell, James Campbell-Prager, Doug Chamberlain, Gary Craswell, Cleone Duncan, Jack Duffy, Susan Ferley, Grace Finley-Stickings, Heidi Ford, Lorraine Foreman, Kassie Hall, David Hughes, Chilina Kennedy, Blanche Lund, Wade Lynch, Janet MacEwen, Duncan Macintosh, Brian Mackay, Peggy Mahon, Tracy Michailidis, Charlotte Moore, Gordon Pinsent, Jamie Ray-Farrar, Dean Regan, Max Reimer, Caroline Smith, Marilyn Stewart, Rowena Stinson, Toby Tarnow, Kathy Thiessen, Jennifer Toulmin, Fen Watkin, Campbell Webster.

Apologies to key people I could not reach and especially to all those who might feel left out of any acknowledgment of their contributions to 44 years of our successful musical. Every single one of you contributed to a phenomenon that has lasted all these years and is heading for its Golden Anniversary. That's exactly half of what dear Lucy Maud has already achieved with her novel.

Enjoy!

Don Harron
January 2008, Toronto.

1 O SOLO ME—OH!

I'm the only one left. The sole survivor of the creative team that put together a musical for the second year of the Charlottetown Festival that has lasted forty-four years based on a novel that is a hundred years old.

Here is the initial creative team.

I adapted the orphan from the world famous novel by Lucy Maud Montgomery.

The score was composed by Norman Campbell, with lyrics by myself, Elaine Campbell and Mavor Moore. It was directed and choreographed by Alan Lund with musical arrangements by John Fenwick. But their turn in this story will come later. First we have to go back to the very beginning

2 NO NO SOLO ME—OH!

Oops! Hold the phone…get me rewrite. I forgot about other souls who have survived to this writing, and contributed significantly to our Anne enterprise from the very start.

For what is a stage musical without sets and costumes? The original designers, costumes by Marie Day and sets by Murray Laufer, a husband and wife team who designed the original production in 1965. Their creations have been maintained to this day, despite an abortive attempt to bring Anne into the 21st century, sometime in the late, late twentieth century.

Nonsense, *"Anne of Green Gables"* belongs in the late nineteenth century. Although finally published in 1908, it took place much earlier in Lucy Maud's imagination. An artistic director of the Festival in the nineties (not his age, but the decade) who shall remain nameless, attempted to bring in fresh and more realistic concepts of design by someone connected with the National Film Board. The designs would have been perfectly acceptable in a film, but distinctly unimaginative on a stage.

3 THERE'S MORE I FORGOT

And then there is my third sin of omission, Fen Watkin (I never did find out what the long form of his first name is) played piano in the Charlottetown pit from the very beginning, and soon took over the stick-waving chores from the original conductor and arranger, John Fenwick. Fen did this job magnificently from 1965 until the summer of 2005 when he finally retired.

Retired? Fen fits the unofficial definition of retirement: you wake up in the morning with nothing to do, and go to bed eighteen hours later with only half of it done.

4 AND MORE SINS OF OMISSION

How could I ignore the presence of Jack MacAndrew, who handled public relations, marketing and advertising from the beginning of *Anne* at the Festival. Starting in 1965 he stayed on for eight years as Alan Lund's co-producer. Not only that, but in 1966 Jack organized an improvised cabaret every night after the show that was not only fun for the audience who wanted more, but turned out to be a real morale booster for the cast.

After talking to him recently, I can add to his resumé the fact that he was let go as the Charlottetown Mall Santa Claus. Possessor of a big beard and an even bigger paunch, he convinced Island kids that he was the genuine article. No reason was given for his dismissal; there was no drunkenness on the job, or obscene belching in front of the little ones. Too late now, he's already lost thirty five pounds due to his diabetes diet. Mind you Jack has always had a reputation as the Graphic grouch from the weekly columns he writes in the Montague newspaper, the Eastern Graphic.

5 LET'S GO BACKSTAGE

The other long term pioneer, who is still there, is backstage crew-chief Roddy Diamond. Rod started out as a seventeen year old usher at the Festival theatre in 1964, graduated to taking tickets, and half way through the season was backstage with the crew. Other ushers who graduated with honors to the main stage of the Festival were Gracie Finley, Anne from 1968 to 1974 and a triumphant return in 1984-5 with two kids in tow, and Janet McEwen, the current Marilla, went from Front of House to Front and Centre.

In Janet's own words: "In the summer of 1967 I saw *Anne of Green Gables*" for the first time. It was touch and go. My small foot had had an altercation with a shovel and suffice it to say, I had been told that I may not be able to attend the long anticipated matinee performance. After much begging and pleading, an aspirin, a big bandage and a fuzzy pink slipper, I was excitedly sitting in an aisle seat in the brand new Confederation Centre of the Arts, watching with eyes wide open and listening with my young ears.

By intermissions I knew what I wanted to be when I grew up and it definitely involved the period character shoes that all the women were wearing. I had a goal. I would be a performer and I would wear those shoes.

From 1977 to 1979, my job was ushering the audiences in the Charlottetown Festival Theatre to experience the homespun magic of *"Anne of Green Gables."* I would stand at the back of the house and soak up the ambiance while watching and learning from some of the best performers in the business. Sherry Flett, Brian McKay, Doug Chamberlain, Elizabeth Mawson to name a few.

But it was Liz Mawson's Marilla Cuthbert that I would sneak into the back of the house to watch on my nights off. Her stern Marilla was discreetly tempered with a sense of humour, but when she sang "The Words" my eyes would fill with tears. I am proud to say that the summer of 2007 marked my second season with the Charlottetown Festival Company in the role of Marilla Cuthbert. I waited thirty years for the opportunity to fulfill my dream of going from Front of House to Front and Centre. And as fate would have it, I not only have the privilege of filling Elizabeth Mawson's shoes, I literally get to wear her very own shoes."

Almost as long as the annals of the Festival is the backstage career of Rick Wilson. He started in 1966 after a career as a university professor, both here and in the United States. Both Roddy and Rick agree that after forty-three seasons it's still fun to work the show even after 3149 performances of *"Anne the Musical."*

6 THE ROAD TO CHARLOTTETTOWN WAS VIA PARRY SOUND

The *Anne* thing really started when the composer of the music, Norman Campbell, loaned me a gray roll-top cardigan sweater he had worn during the war years on Sable Island.

It was the first week of September 1952 and the first season of CBC television. Norman was busy directing a puppet show called "Uncle Chichimus" This puppet was created by puppeteer John Conway and it looked very much like the man in charge of CBC television, Mavor Moore. John, Mavor and I had all been post-war members of Dora Mavor Moore's Village Players, soon to become a professional unit called The New Play Society. Mavor insisted, but I voted against, going professional. Fortunately I was outvoted. (Mavor created the lyrics for three of the best numbers in our *Anne* musical, but as I said, that comes later.) Norman envisioned another puppet on the show called Mavor Moose, but that was not to be.

I was in the next studio rehearsing a monologue for CBC TV's first variety show, The Big Revue. I was playing a character I had created earlier that year in Spring Thaw '52, an annual revue that started in 1948, featuring a satirical slant on things Canadian. I had been involved in the first four of these outings, and had been fairly unsuccessful making my fellow Canadian laugh at their foibles and follies.

The star of Spring Thaw, a very wise woman called Jane Mallett said to me "You're too young to be criticizing the government. People think you're just being a smart ass. What you need is a disguise, a mask, become an older character who will have the authority of long experience."

Are you still with me on this? Because it was two years before I got around to doing it.

After "Spring Thaw 1950," I went on a three week vacation in London, England, got a job in the play "A Streetcar Named Desire," the second day I arrived and stayed for two years. One of the high points of my theatre-going career was going to the London Palladium to see the great Lena Horne. Her opening act was Bernard Miles. The character actor (e.g. Joe Gargery in Great Expectations) later founded his own theatre and became Lord Miles. But in 1951 he was shuffling on stage as an old Essex farmer pushing a huge wagon wheel that looked like it was coated with pigeon droppings. He looked out at the audience and said in his rural accent "Oi found this, Oim gonna take ee ome and mike a ladder outen it!"

It was a moment of revelation comparable for me to the experience of the Apostle Paul on the road to Damascus. (I exaggerate. What did you expect? I'm an actor) All through my stay in London, I had seen and met Canadians with that look on their faces as if they were gazing at a distant horizon in a blaze of fierce sunshine. Eyes scrunched up and mouth perpetually open. Those were my people, I thought, and there was a time back in 1942 when I had been one of them, a son of toil covered in a ton of soil. It was the summer of '42 and I signed on as a hired man rather than write those Grade Thirteen exams. The man I worked for was my mother's second cousin and he wore a peak cap, glasses and a grey cardigan sweater.

Where is all this going? You may well ask.

I returned to Canada in the spring of 1952 and was re-hired for the latest edition of Spring Thaw by its creator, director, composer and lyricist, the very same Mavor Moore who, later that year, was to launch Canadian Television. Because I had been gone for a long while in another country, Canadians thought that I might have become a star. That's what Mavor was counting on.

"Harron," he said " I'm going to star you in this year's Spring Thaw."

"But Mavor" I said "I can neither sing nor dance"

"Oh God, don't I know it" he replied "but why not write one of those monologues you tried to do last time you were with us."

"About what" I said

He shrugged and said "Ohhhh…make it something you know something about!"

I have a painful memory of a moment during Spring Thaw 1950 when Mavor got furious at something I had ad-libbed on stage during one of my would-be topical monologues. The papers that day were full of the announcement that Evita Peron would be coming to Toronto for cancer treatments. So dumb-and-dumber Don Harron announced "that Argentina was sending its first class meat to Toronto to be cured."

It was the only time I ever had a harsh word from the man who was really the artistic mentor of many of us, although he was barely five years older than me. Mavor had tried to turn me into a stage director by handing me the world premiere of John Coulter's play about Louis Riel, with Mavor in the title role. Faced with a play that had fourteen different sets, and over twenty characters, I simply staged it the way we had been staging Spring Thaw: first scene downstage, second scene upstage and so on ad infinitum.

The main problem I had was with the actor playing the title character. Besides being the head of our New Play Society, Mavor also had a job with the United Nations Radio in New York. Consequently he was absent for most of the rehearsals. It was a couple of days before opening night when Mavor finally came back to us with only the haziest recollection of his many, many lines of dialogue.

Opening night was also the world premiere of a play about two men who shaped the direction of Canadian history, John A. MacDonald and Louis Riel.

As John A., Bob Christie was line perfect, and it was a role he continued to play for the rest of his career. But Mavor was still struggling with his lines.

The set on which Riel was later to be hanged was a platform with room underneath to crawl under. That's where I spent the evening, with script in hand, whispering the lines to Mavor. We got away with it. When he was hanged, the Te Deum was sung by four young choristers from St. Michael's college. Mavor had persuaded Monsignor Ronan to lend him these young men who sang like angels. (They later became known as "The Four Lads"). As Mavor swung from the gallows the curtain closed on a standing ovation and The Four Lads, unheard over the applause, sang an up-tempo version of "Tell Me How Long the Train's Bin Gone."

At the tender of age of thirty, Mavor had the audacity to take on the role of King Lear. This time the U.N. didn't get in the way, but his throat did. He threw himself so much into the first day of rehearsal that he blew his throat cracking his cheeks on the windy heath. He went to bed with laryngitis. We had ten days to rehearse Shakespeare's greatest tragedy and Mavor was absent for eight of them. He must have spent the time in bed memorizing his part, because on opening night he was line perfect.

More than that, he proved he could ad lib the Bard in perfect iambic pentameter. There is a scene on the blasted heath when Lear and his jester enter a little hovel to escape from the storm. The hovel contains nothing but a stool, which the now-crazed Lear identifies as one of his errant daughters, Regan. However on opening night there was no stool there. Mavor looked offstage and noticed that our stage manager was sitting on it, blissfully unaware of the crisis he was creating onstage. This didn't faze Mavor Moore. He turned to his jester, played by a very young Jack Medhurst and said: "Where is the stool, Fool?" Medhurst gave him back the equivalent of DUH! So Mavor pointing to the stage manager in the wings said: "Arise and bring me yonder joint stool. And you and I shall jointly sit upon't!" Anyone who can ad lib in iambic pentameter with an apostrophe in it to boot, gained my undying respect.

Whatever Mavor wants, Mavor gets.

(Have patience with my tangents. Mavor Moore was a vital force in the re-emergence of the musical of *Anne of Green Gables*.)

Trusting that Mavor had forgotten my remark about Evita Peron, I set about to do his bidding. My thoughts about a monologue turned to that venerable institution the Canadian National Exhibition. I had worked there the summer before I went on the farm. And combined with my actual farm experience and my memories of men with white foreheads and red necks in blue suits that were a trifle too short in the leg, I decided to do a monologue about an Ontario farmer visiting the CNE.

I borrowed a blue serge suit of my father's that was too short in the leg for both him and me. I put on an Indian headdress provided by Lowney's chocolate people I still hear the piercing cry of: "Six bars, a hat and a bag, all fer twenny five cents!" echoing thru the halls of the 'The Poor Fud Bilding" as Charlie called it.

Anyway, to make a long story even longer, (whatever happened to *"Anne of Green Gables"*) my monologue called Th'Ex was greeted by roars of laughter. I don't think it was the jokes I tried to write that caused the uproar, as much as it was the fact that my audience had never heard an authentic Ontario accent on any stage. It was what the critic Edmund Wilson called "the shock of Recognition."

Still with me? (I appreciate such loyalty).

When it came to repeating my Spring Thaw monologue, on the first weekly edition of Canadian television's Big Revue, I was positioned beside a rural mail-box, and told to tell the audience about my visit to the CNE. But I didn't have the proper costume for everyday farm apparel.

I was about to panic when I passed by the studio next door. In rehearsal was a nightly television show that included a weather report on a blackboard by a man called Percy Saltzman who ended by tossing the chalk high into the air and never missing a catch. But what caught my eye were two members of the production team who were in a huddle about the soon-to-be produced fifteen minute live television show. The air of excitement was palpable.

Those first months of CBC television in the fall of 1952 will never be forgotten by anyone who participated. Television was in a ferment in those days and most people involved in it worked eighteen to twenty hours day. The pulse was frantic as we rushed from show to show in a dizzying round of shows and rehearsals. Often the day would start at an eight a.m. rehearsal and a nine a.m. radio broadcast to Ontario schools. I remember once playing a scene from Hamlet, and I was so full of sleep that instead of saying "I do not set my life at a pin's fee…" I blurted out "I do not set my life at a Finn's pee." If they had been awake and listening, the kids must have hooted.

After the school broadcast, I would go to a rehearsal of GM theatre, a weekly hour-long play. Then I would go home and try to write the next

Charlie monologue for the Big Revue. I remember the very opening show, the CBC logo came on upside down, and the Boyd gang had robbed three banks in a row the same day and escaped, which allowed Charlie to say "I hear some banks in Trawntuh wuz rob by outside parties. Makes a change!"

But back to the little studio next door to the one that housed the Big Revue. The only reason I walked in was because the director, Norman Campbell who was on the floor giving advice to a puppet was wearing a grey cardigan sweater.

That sweater was very similar to the one I had seen on my Ontario farmer in 1942, and almost identical to the one worn by the Saskatchewan farmer I worked for, when University students were summoned to Regina and Moosejaw and other parts of Saskatchewan, to help bring in the Big Haircut, the only decent crop the West had since the balmy days of the late twenties. I walked in on my Chaplin farmer (sixty miles west of Moosejaw) as he was eating his breakfast of cold baloney and potatoes, and wearing a cardigan, cap and glasses just like my Ontario farmer. I thought to myself, "My gawd, are they franchising them now?"

Back in that studio I saw something else beside a familiar looking sweater. Someone was pushing a dolly (don't get excited, it's a technical term for the guy who helped move a camera around) and he was wearing a peak cap that was a dead-ringer for the ones worn by both my Ontario and Saskatchewan farmers. I also recognized the wearer of the cap. I had gone to University with him. We had both appeared in the first post-war All Varsity Revue at the University of Toronto, Norman Jewison.

When I was in England writing comedy for Bernard Braden on the BBC, Norman Jewison was also trying his luck with the BBC as a comedy writer on a TV variety show called Starlight Hour. We reconnected happily and eventually Norman became a baby-sitter for our first born, Martha, who arrived in May of 1951. I remember Normie watching Randolph Turpin fighting Sugar Ray Robinson with such intensity that he didn't notice my baby daughter's overflowing diaper while she sat on his knee. (Will this orgy of reminiscence ever get to the point?)

My memory must be playing tricks. I can't remember Norman Jewison being just a crew member pushing a camera, (actually he was Norman Campbell's studio director) but you never know. Everybody did everything in those days. So based on our previous acquaintance I felt emboldened to go up to Norman Jewison and asked if I could borrow his cap. Norman (the Jewison one) hesitated. It was his father's cap and Percy Jewison wore it to pull his cukes in the summer garden at Lefroy, Ontario. I promised to return the cap the next day. He took it off and cheerfully handed it to me.

I had never met the owner of the grey sweater which was so perfect for my purposes. So Norman One introduced me to Norman Two, the director of the show, who was in frantic mid-rehearsal. But Campbell was generous and explain to me that he wore this sweater during the war when he was working as a meteorologist on Sable Island. I made some lame joke that he probably got the wool off the backs of the ponies. He loaned it to me, I think, to get rid of me while he concentrated on the deadline of a live TV show.

Later that season Norman Campbell directed a sketch I wrote for The Big Revue, a take-off on science fiction space adventures sponsored by a breakfast cereal called Space Puffs (which contained nothing but air) and I found that this director was a real ham of a performer with boundless energy and enthusiasm. I looked forward to working with him again.

The upshot of this early encounter was that I borrowed the sweater and cap of the two Normans and promised fervently to return both items the next day. I never did. Fifty five years later I am still wearing them on stage as Charlie Farquharson. The hat now looks air conditioned and the sweater is about seventy percent replaced with repairs.

(Yes, yes but when do we get back to Green Gables?)

Move back to 1952 and then forward to 1955. I am co-starring with former Spring Thaw star Jane Mallett in a fall revue called "Fine Frenzy." We were going to call it "Fall Freeze" but we felt that Spring Thaw might object. I was wearing both Normans cap and sweater in a monologue about swimming across Lake Ontario. That was the year a fourteen year old called Marilyn Bell had managed this difficult feat. Charlie Farquharson planned to cross the waters near Niagara-on-the-Lake where it was less that two miles across. Under his sweater he wore long underwear which had been soaked (he said) in Crown Brand Corn Syrup to ward off frigidity. My opening line was, "I plan to start acrost as soon as she's cam."

Backstage after the show I received a visit from Norman and Elaine Campbell.

Norman had come to visit his sweater. I was so glad he brought Elaine along because she had the most infectious and uproarious laugh I had ever heard this side of Ethel Merman; she was a one-person laugh machine. But Norman had another purpose in mind beside asking for his sweater back. This seemed to get lost in the shuffle when he announced that CBC television had offered him 90 minutes of television time to do with whatever he wished. Can you imagine such a thing happening today, when the only numbers the CBC are interested in now have dollar signs in front of them?

I had seen one of the musicals that Norman and Elaine created for TV, an Eric Nicol script called "We Took to the Woods," starring Robert Goulet and Sharon Acker. I assumed the talented pair would dream up another such venture. (Norman and Elaine, not Bob and Sharon.)

No way. The composer and his lyricist wife were stumped for a project. They mentioned the earliest Canadian stage musical they had seen was in Vancouver back in 1950 at Theatre Under the Stars. It was called "Timber" and had been written by Doug Nixon and Dolores Claman, (who lives in England now but is famous for writing the famous Hockey Night in Canada song we hear every Saturday night.)

The Campbells were asking me if I had any suggestions for a musical for television. I told them I had been reading a book to my two tiny daughters Martha and Mary. They were enjoying it tremendously partly because I didn't interfere with the author's words by making fun of the story, the way I usually did with well-known fairy tales.

My two daughters have since gone on to flourish in our profession. Martha wrote my biography "A Parent Contradiction" and is issuing a volume of children's poems written for her nieces Ruby and Ella. Mary, their mother, is busy writing and directing her own screenplays which include "I Shot Andy Warhol" "American Psycho" "The Notorious Betty Page." She is presently involved in a film for Paramount about a teenage vampire in an exclusive girls school.

You guessed it, the book I was reading to these two tots was *Anne of Green Gables* by Lucy Maud Montgomery. (Whew, only took me a few pages to get to the point).

I suggested to the Campbells that it would make a good TV musical because the heroine has such an imagination that the only way to render her expressive bursts in a dramatic form would be to set them to music.

Norman remembered seeing a film version back in the thirties and promised to look into it right away. He never did. Norman was caught up in many

Anne of Green Gables the Musical ~ 101 Things you didn't know

more TV projects than just puppet shows. I wrote and performed in sketches for him on editions of "The Big Revue." He was an absolute joy to work with. His constant enthusiasm was positively addictive. Norman didn't have time to read novels, too busy, as he was one of the producer's on CBC's Folio, a weekly show often ninety minutes long. But his wife Elaine found time to get the novel out of the library and was as delighted by it as my young daughters. That was enough for Norman and the project was a go.

7 ANOTHER GREEN GABLES DETOUR! (Via Stratford)

One of the reasons Canadian have been succesful in television south of the border is because we are all pioneers in this business and we only survive due to a compulsive versatility. Most of us have done everything in this business because we have to. I have directed, produced, acted, designed a set, swept the stage, even appeared in a ballet and an opera. I must qualify that the ballet was conceived by Alan Lund for my "History of Canada Spring Thaw" with Alan recreating the Battle of the Plains of Abraham as two basketball teams, blue for the French and red for the British. The score varied each night. The opera was at Stratford in Wolf Ferrari's "The Evils of Tobacco" with Mary Lou Fallis and Gary Relyea and thankfully I was cast as a mute. Enough of this nonsense. Canadians get by in North America because they are willing and able to adjust to anything.

In November of 1955 I started work on the libretto, eager to adapt the orphan *"Anne of Green Gables."* Originally I had been hired to appear in a play in London's West End that fall. I got the call to do the part during my third season at Stratford, Ontario. It was opening night of Tyrone Guthrie's production of "The Merchant of Venice," and I was resting at home preparing for the nervous ordeal when the phone rang and a voice said: "Hello Donald Harron, this is Walter Kerr of the Herald Tribune…" I presumed it was that juvenile joker Bill Shatner, who was playing Gratiano to my Bassanio, giving me the business just before our opening night. I shouted "Goddam it Shatner, go learn your bloody lines before you forget them like you did at dress rehearsal."

The voice at the other end said politely "Nevertheless, Donald Harron, this is still Walter Kerr of the Herald Tribune, and my wife Jean wants to offer you a part in the London production of her play." He didn't have to tell me the name. I had seen Jean Kerr's "King of Hearts" on Broadway when I

17

was there that season doing an Irish play called "Home is the Hero." (Chris Plummer insisted on calling it Here is the Homo). I had seen Jean's play during the fall season and was delighted by its humour. A little boy is invited to stay for lunch, and feels he should phone his mother first. He makes the request to Mum and a long silence follows. He slowly puts down the phone and says sadly "I had lunch."

I was to replace former child star Jackie Cooper in the original cast and join the current stars Donald Cook and Cloris Leachman (of the Mary Tyler Moore show and later the Teutonic housekeeper in Mel Brooks film "Young Frankenstein." ("Fronkensteen? He voss mine boy-friend.") Unfortunately the upshot of this whole exciting prospect was that shortly after my Walter Kerr phone call, our star Donald Cook suddenly passed away and the London production of the play was just as suddenly canceled. Two days later Norman and Elaine visited me backstage in my dressing room. So I found myself completely at liberty to attempt something I had never tried before, an adaptation of a book considered a classic all over the world, for the musical stage.

I had had my baptism in the field of literary adaptation for television when I wrote thirteen scripts for a twenty-six series in the first season of Canadian TV. They were based on another world-famous Canadian classic novel, Stephen Leacock's "Sunshine Sketches of a Little Town." Both Leacock and Lucy Maud Montgomery had created such a following in the decade before the first World War that although there were Europeans who had no idea where Canada was, they were faithful readers of both Canadian novels.

I approached this assignment accompanied by the advice of a master of adaptation, Canadian humorist Tommy Tweed, who told me "there is only one rule of adaptation: be true to your author." Some people think that the jokes in our Anne musical are mine, ninety-nine percent of the time they originated with Lucy Maud herself.

To prepare for the task I had read a book called The Art of Dramatic Writing by a man called Lajos Egri. I knew nothing about him before or since, but the one thing I remember from that book was a simple directive: if you are going to write a play you should be able to describe the essence of it in one sentence.

Mark Twain had described *"Anne of Green Gables"* as the dearest heroine in fiction since Alice in Wonderland. I went even further back to get my one sentence evaluation of the plot. *Anne* was the re-creation of the basic heroine of all time, Cinderella, orphaned by the death of her father she faces life with a cruel step-mother and two indifferent step-sisters but eventually aided by a fairy godmother.

"Anne of Green Gables" didn't have a fairy godmother, but she did have a sympathetic ally in the shy bachelor Matthew Cuthbert. Basically she was on her own in life's struggles. My one sentence capsule version of Lucy Maud Montgomery's novel: the perpetual loser emerges as the winner.

8 IS THERE A DRAFT IN HERE?

The first problem I faced was that the original novel deals with a little girl of about eleven years of age who ends the book as a young woman closing in on eighteen. This doesn't work in dramatic form. You have to use the same actress throughout.

The solution? Ignore all specific references to the passage of time. Concentrate on the four seasons; never mention the ticking of a clock and the passage of years.

Anne arrives on the island in the spring, has a summer full of ice-cream and falling off the roof, returns to school in the fall, resumes rivalries with Gilbert and Josie Pye, has more quirky adventures involving green hair dye, getting her best friend Diana drunk accidentally, then spends most of the winter studying for a scholarship. The cutting of her hair after the green dye episode allows her to go from pig-tailed urchin to a bobbed-hair mature teenager. The story itself goes from spring to spring ending in a mixture of triumph (the scholarship) and tragedy (Matthew's death).

In about three weeks I turned out a first draft script of some forty five pages, figuring the lyrics to the songs would fill out the rest of the ninety minutes. So far the adaptation has been done by myself in isolation. Now came the fun part.

The three of us, Norman and Elaine and myself, gathered in their home at 20 George Henry Boulevard in Willowdale, a suburb of Toronto. At the time they were a childless couple, the only other live item on the premises was a big chow dog named Puff. But Elaine was already showing signs of impending motherhood, and if she was eating for two, she seemed intent on cooking for four because she kept Norman and myself (particularly a glutton like me) well fed at all times.

Despite all this extra activity, Elaine was able to project new lyrics from the depths of her kitchen into the living room where Norman presided at the piano, inventing tunes that seemed to me to come forth from him effortlessly. Elaine said she would sometimes throw a lyric idea at him while he was shaving with an electric razor, and the razor became sometimes the accompaniment to his fertile musical ideas. Norman may have made his reputation as a producer and director but he was a natural performer, and delighted in every opportunity to show it.

Elaine said that when Norman seemed to be noodling around on the piano it did not sound like noodling to her. She said he was playing whole phrases that would be easy to put words to. The tunes were already written in his head and she could hear whole sentences of the lyrics-to-be when he played. He hadn't yet had time to read the book but depended on Elaine's descriptions. He could write songs just from knowing the title we suggested. He would then play a whole piece through with nothing but the title in mind, and from that Elaine would write yards of lyrics to end up with the line "Gee I'm Glad I'm No One Else But Me."

Elaine wrote the bubbly girlie lyrics and I wrote the middle part of the song, all about the vicious strife between the Island tribes that stained the soil with blood and turned it forever red.

More than once I fell asleep on the sofa, too full of Elaine's treats to stay awake, but my two colleagues continued their collaboration, too polite to rouse me from my slumbers. At one point, according to Elaine, Puff the magic chow dog approached me supine on the sofa and proceeded to lick my face with his huge purple tongue. This was not enough to rouse me from my sleep. Norman claimed that all I did was react in my sleep with a big smile and a chorus of Yes! Yes! Yes.

9 WORKING LONG DISTANCE

The lyrics writing continued between the three of us, but most of it had to be conducted on the long distance phone between Toronto and New York. We were part-timers in the field of musicals. Norman was still inundated with shows to do at the CBC and I was still trying to renew my career in New York. I had already appeared in three Broadway shows, but the immigration rules had changed and I was in the process of attempting to get my green card. In the meantime, I was lying my way across the border to accept television shows like the U.S. Steel Hour, Producer's Showcase, and Lamp Unto My Feet.

Eventually I solved my dilemma by bribing an employee at the U.S. Embassy in Toronto. It cost me seven hundred and fifty bucks. I understand the going rate now is about fifteen thousand. I went to the New York Public library just off Forty Second Street to research the turn-of-the-century method of making ice-cream. A lot of lore was later discarded but we hoped this was going to be the big number that the kids would be humming long after the curtain came down.

When I got a chance to play a leading role opposite Joanne Woodward (with Joan Blondell as my mother) I decided I would try to write some lyrics between rehearsals and send them by teletype through the CBC's New York office situated in the United Nations Building. I did this more than once and attempted to check Norman and Elaine's reactions to my lyrics on the long distance phone. Many times I wasn't able to reach Norman because of his television duties but Elaine was always there.

Somehow none of my lyrics ever got through, and the script deadline loomed. The phone calls between me and the Campbells started to get frantic. So I checked with the CBC rep in New York, Vincent Tovell. He claims he had sent the song lyrics I had written, and couldn't figure out why they never arrived. The answer came in the headlines of New York newspapers. Senator Joe McCarthy and his committee had been investigating the UN for Communist influence and finding it. Through Vincent Tovell we found that they had pounced on and censored the lyrics I had tried to send to Toronto because of the scurrilous words…red sands…red soil…red hair.

10 GIVING BIRTH TO LYRICS

Eventually my words got there, including the lyrics for Anne's apology to Mrs. Lynde which consisted of two long verses, the first with every one of its thirteen lines rhyming in Lynde, wind, sinned, the other verse of eleven lines all rhyming in airy, solitary, salutary. Norman's cryptic comment upon receipt of this was "Harron you are so ignorant about music that you invent new forms." After many tries, Norman finally set it to music by doing a pretty good imitation of Puccini.

Elaine kept on writing lyrics even though by now she was heavily pregnant with her first child. Norm claimed that she was even writing "Gee I'm Glad I'm No-One Else But Me" in the delivery room, while waiting for first son Robin to appear. When Norman came to visit his wife after the happy

Leisa Way, Lorraine Foreman,
"THE APOLOGY"

arrival, he congratulated her first on… "the excellent lyrics" she had manage to write in extremis, and second on becoming the mother of their new baby. Norman says "we didn't clearly request a boy, but we're happy with the one we got."

11 MAKING ARRANGEMENTS

Norman arranged for someone to do the musical arrangements for his score, while I was busy in New York being Joanne Woodward's husband on a U.S. Steel Hour television show. There was a young fellow who came after rehearsals to take Joanne to dinner before he went to do his own theatre performance.

His name… Paul Newman. He was playing the good and well-mannered young man but dull suitor to Janice Rule who loses the girl to a hunky Ralph Meeker, in a William Inge play called "Picnic," He was of course, on the brink of becoming the movie hunk of all time. (I mean Paul Newman, not Ralph Meeker.)

The author of the teleplay, James Costigan (I can't remember the name of his teleplay that I was in) was a help with my Anne adaptation. I would come to his shabby apartment after rehearsal and the first thing he did was to grab a huge fly swatter and flail vigorously at the myriad cockroaches on his kitchen table. Cockroaches scattered, we sat down and I listened to his sound advice about adaptation. Jimmy got so enthused about my project that he even contributed some school yard lyrics that we later abandoned.

Where was I? Oh yes. Back in Toronto, Norman hired the dean of Canadian Jazz, Phil Nimmons to take us back to the turn of the century Prince Edward Island. I thought it was an odd choice. True these were the classical stalwarts of the CBC Radio Orchestra: Gordon Kushner conducting, Leo Barkin on piano, Jon Duncan on the harp, Sammy Hershenhorn on violin, and there were also some real swingers in the ensemble: Moe Koffman on clarinet, Murray Ginsberg on trombone, Ellis McClintock on trumpet, Mickey Shannon on drums, and Gurney Titmarsh on bass. (Fellow musicians always referred to Gurney as Moffat Boobswamp! EXPLANATION: Gurney was a make of oven, and Moffat did the same in another range.)

But my conservative concerns were swept away when I heard them play the Phil Nimmons's score. He served Norm Campbell's melodies to a T and took us back to a turn-of-the-century Prince Edward Island with a simple rural approach to Norman's tunes and Lucy Maud's lovely words rendered into lyrics by Elaine and myself.

There was no possibility of the actor-singers pre-recording with the orchestra. The singers would record a cappella, and Norman had the job of making the orchestra sync with a pre-recorded bunch of vocals.

Ahhh, those dear dead days of live television!

12 CASTING ON THE FLY

Casting was completed soon after I got back from New York.

Marilla Cuthbert, Anne's old maid (it was a politically correct term back in 1955) guardian was to be played by Margot Christie. I had been with Margot and her husband Robert in the New Play Society repertory company of Dora Mavor Moore. English-born, she and Bob had been part of Tyrone Guthrie's Old Vic company production of Hamlet before the war. It was completely in modern dress and starred Alec Guiness as Hamlet. Margot had a stern face and an authoritarian voice, and I thought she was perfect for the part.

Even more perfect (if such a phrase can be considered correct) was the casting of her bachelor brother Matthew. John Drainie had been considered by more than one source as the greatest radio actor in the world, incredibly versatile in a dazzling array of roles. In a visual medium, like stage and television, he was limited by a highly visible limp. But as Matthew Cuthbert this only added to his endearing vulnerability. I was overjoyed that he accepted the role.

The role of the central character, Anne Shirley, was won by a nice Jewish girl from Gravelbourg, Saskatchewan, called Toby Tarnow.

What would Maritime Lucy Maud have thought of that? Toby had already played Anne in a radio adaptation and won an award for it and at the

Toby Tarnow looking out the window.

time she was quite busy as Princess Winterfall Summerspring on my little girls' favorite television show at the time, which they persisted in calling Howdy Doo-doo. She busted her nether parts to make all rehearsals, despite a hectic schedule.

Gilbert Blythe, the boy who pulled Anne's braid and called her Carrots on her first day of school, was Bill Cole, a young actor who had been with me in the third season at Stratford, Ontario. I had heard his singing in the shower and suggested him to director Norman, producer Norman, composer Norman and co-lyricist Norman.

For Anne's best friend, Diana Barry, (we will be bosom friends till death do it to our parts) Norman chose young Nonnie Griffin because he felt she had a period turn-of-the-century Gibson girl face. She did, and she also had one of the most spectacular busts upon this earth. I know first hand (oops! better rephrase that) I knew from recent experience because I had been in a production of Tennessee Williams, "The Glass Menagerie" and Nonnie played my ailing, pale, wan, crippled sister whose only recreation in life was collecting the glass animals in the above mentioned menagerie. Anyway the girl had to be strapped in hard to hide the obvious protuberances. I hoped Norman would see his way to do the same again with the same young lady or our show might turn out to be a complete bust.

13 ABSENTEE ME

I missed almost all the rehearsals because I had to return to New York to play a role in…oh what's his name…Twilight Zone…Rod Serling. He had written a multi-cast television script called "Tragedy in a Temporary Town." It was about a racist incident involving the hazing of a Puerto Rican youth by a bunch of louts. I was one of the louts. My older brother was the macho actor Jack Warden, whose job was to smack me in the face. He refrained from doing this all through rehearsals, which was a great relief to me, until the actual TV transmission when he unwound a blow upside my head that had me seeing all the stars of the Milky Way for the next fifteen minutes. The big thing that came out of this show, was the star, Lloyd Bridges, forgetting his lines. As the anti-racist hero his job was to take a sledge-hammer and smash all the glaring lights of the assembled trucks of the bigots. The exhilaration of doing all this damage made dear Lloyd forget what he was suppose to say, so he reverted to some good old fashioned cussing. It was mild by today's standards. The most salacious thing he managed to say was "Goddamit," but it earned him the front page in next day's New York Times. (Are you getting diversion-itis by now? Sorry.)

Meanwhile back at the Anne ranch, things were coming along just fine. A recent addition to the cast was another member of the Howdy Doo-Doo clan. Barbara Hamilton played the fey witch Willow on that series, but there was nothing fey about her portrayal of Lucilla, the clerk in Blair's store. She accosts poor Matthew and backs him up against the wheels of the coffee bean-grinding machine to find out exactly what it is that he wants to buy. (Puffed sleeves.) That scene remains my most vivid memory of the whole enterprise.

There were two weeks rehearsal, of which two days were in the studio for the actual show. Day one, in the studio, was for blocking with cameras. Day two, in the studio, was a dress rehearsal with orchestra, which was brought in only on show day for a three hour call, with some very fast conducting. For the rehearsals the cast had pianist Gordon Kushner. On show day actors and musicians were in different studios and there was no monitor for conductor Gordon. The whole enterprise must have been based on faith.

14 OPENING NIGHT AND CLOSING NIGHT

The thing about live television where opening night is closing night, is that there is no turning back. None of that "OK people, let's try that one again." No sirree Bob. The live show itself is recorded on a kinescope and packed off to Winnipeg and Vancouver.

The live telecast was the equivalent of a D-Day landing. One chance and that's it.

Our Anne, Toby had been a pillar of strength during rehearsals and bonding wonderfully with her Bosom Friend Diana Barry (now well strapped in).

On show day, Toby had eaten something that disagreed with her. Some form of food poisoning had affected her throat. She was given a black carbon pill to induce her to throw up. It got stuck half way down. Buckets were placed at strategic spots in the studio in case she did throw up. As we started the dress rehearsal, our *"Anne of Green Gables"* couldn't utter a sound, much less sing our lyrics. To add to the tension, Nonnie Griffin, as Diana, came into rehearsal with a case of pneumonia. Her doctor forbade her to do our show, but true trooper, she was there anyway. Did I mention that the orchestra was in another building, actually in a radio studio? I phoned leader Gordon Kushner recently to find out how he relayed the cues to the performers in their studio, but the dear man had passed away two months ago. The arranger, Phil Nimmons, wasn't with us in the studio, he was probably playing jazz in some bistro. With Norman Campbell gone I may never know how the cues were relayed from conductor to director to actor.

CBC Archives

back row: *Gladys Forrester, Phil Nimmons,* front row: *Don Harron, Toby Tarnow, John Drainie, Norman Campbell*

With Toby a complete mute I was panicking, but Norm Campbell was cucumberish cool and told her to just mouth the words so he could rehearse all the camera positions for the actual show which would take place in a few hours time. A lot of this remains a blur to me. All I know is that this little girl from Gravelbourg Saskatchewan, was absolutely heroic (or is the word heroine-oic) that day in the studio. On the show, Toby Tarnow gave a full fledged, full voiced performance. Where the voice came from I couldn't tell you but you can see and hear it for yourself because the CBC now sells this 90 minutes black and white special made in the spring of 1956.

(Norman & Elaine admitted to me that old kinescopes of our Anne musical were smuggled into the United States wrapped in diapers. Nothing like a pampered heroine.)

15 ENDGAME

I understand the reviews for the show were very friendly,

The next day I was on a train back to New York as I had to start rehearsing a ninety minute television show. This was the NBC Producer's Showcase Special of "The Barretts of Wimpole Street," starring Catherine Cornell as Elizabeth Barrett and Anthony Quayle as Robert Browning. I was cast as Elizabeth Barrett's youngest brother, Octavius, with an unruly cowlick and an endearing stammer. I had worked with Catherine Cornell on tour and on Broadway two years before, in Christopher Fry's "The Dark is Light Enough," and she was very friendly-motherly toward this young Canadian actor. On opening night in New York she ordered champagne for the entire cast. To express my appreciation I remember saying "Thank you for this Miss Cornell. It must be the ginger-ale of champagnes." I wasn't trying to be funny, I was just that dumb. Miss Cornell forgave my gaff and insisted I be in the cast in this two hour television special. Tony Quayle I had seen in Stratford on Avon in the role of Falstaff to Richard Burton's Prince Hal in "Henry IV Part One." We shared a lot of anecdotes about being in the Bard.

Years later, in the early seventies, I met him again in Knoxville Tennessee (that's Dolly Parton Country; she once said that "I came down from the hills of Tennessee and brought them with me). At that time Tony Quayle had been summoned from England to help the University of Tennessee take over an old burlesque house and turn it into a classical repertory theatre. There was a fund-raising variety show to get the theatre started, and I had come from the Hee-Haw studio in Nashville dressed in my Charlie Farquharson costume. Anthony Quayle approached me with an air of caution. "Excuse me, but are you Donald Harron of Stratford-on-Tario?" I nodded. "Yes Tony and we appeared on TV together with Catherine Cornell." Tony stared open-mouthed at my unshaven face surmounted by Norman Jewison's father's tattered hat and Norm Campbell's ancient Sable Island cardigan. He said to me with horror in his voice "Good God man, then how did you come to be dressed like this?" I replied "Just lucky I guess."

16 INTERREGNUM

"Anne of Green Gables" on television was my farewell to Canada for ten years. A lot of Canadians are under the impression that I am one of those stout nationalists who would never leave their native soil to work for foreigners. Not true.

I have lived and worked in England four different times, 1950-1, 1953-4, 1963-4 and 1969-70. I spent ten years in New York theatre and five years in California-based television. I had very little contact with Norman and Elaine, but they continued with their mutual collaboration, including a television musical with Toby Robins and Inge Swenson, based on the play "She Stoops to Conquer," with the not yet politically incorrect title of "The Gay Deceivers."

I came back to Canada occasionally to see my parents and do guest shots on TV.

The thing that eventually brought me back to this country was the success of the stage version of *"Anne of Green Gables."*

Each time I returned Stateside, I usually brought a little bit of Canada back with me in the form of a book. In 1956, I picked up a paperback copy of Earle Birney's World War II novel "Turvey." That summer, while rehearsing the English hit "Separate Tables," as the only Canadian member of an all-British cast, I found that the rehearsals were so sparse that I had time on my hands to adapt Birney's novel into a three-act play, the cast had all done the play for two years in London. "Turvey" is a delightful comic novel about a Canadian sad sack who is desperate to be all-over-active in World War II and continually frustrated in his efforts.

I wrote two acts while our play "Separate Tables" was on the road in Princeton and Boston and I finished the third act after our successful opening on Broadway. I sent the play "Turvey" to my perennial theatre guru Mavor Moore, and it seems to me that he booked it into a theatre immediately. It opened in January of 1957 and I was desperate to see it on stage in Toronto. My contract with "Separate Tables" wouldn't allow me to see it, according to the producer Robert Whitehead, who happened to be a Canadian. I called him on that, said he was holding back the cause of our native theatre by not allowing a would-be playwright to view his own work. He laughed and gave me the night off to go to Toronto to see a wonderful Canadian actor, Douglas Rain, in the title role of Turvey. Doug had been my understudy the first-season at Stratford, Ontario, but I made goddam sure he never got on to replace me.

Whatever happened to *"Anne of Green Gables,"* the Musical?

Not much.

Two years after we had that one night stand, the CBC requested that the show be re-created anew rather than repeat via kinescope. The original Anne, Toby Tarnow, was busy having a baby; Cathy Willard took her place. I never saw the repeat creation but I understand that she did a good job. Norman was too busy doing other shows to have a look at the 1956 production. The re-creation of the musical was in 1958 and nothing else happened until 1964.

17 HOLLYWOOD AND NOT SO FINE

By that time I was a denizen of Hollywood, living off television acting jobs on Burke's Law, 12 O'Clock High, Dr. Kildare, Outer Limits, etc. Never comedy, not even a sign of a smirk. I was told by a casting director that I had a serious face. I replied: "So does Buster Keaton." Charlie Farquharson didn't exist except when I got back to Canada to do a TV guest spot.

I had an unusual experience when I was auditioning for the part of John Wilkes Booth for Desilu's production of "The Diary of Samuel Mudd," the Maryland doctor who unknowingly fixed the broken leg of Abraham Lincoln's assassin. The director said to me "I don't know your work Mr. Harron but I did manage to catch your father on Canadian television." My father? Dear Lionel Harron who worked at the Ontario Department of Highways but was now at home, retired, playing his mandolin? No this Desilu guy thought Charlie Farquharson was my father. Anyway he was impressed enough with Charlie to give me the part. I got a chance to assassinate a Republican.

By 1964, the next time *"Anne of Green Gables"* reappeared in my life, I was attempting to be a Hollywood writer as well as an actor. I sent scripts to The Dick Van Dyke Show, and a Burl Ives series called O.K. Crackerby. He played an old eccentric millionaire who tried to govern his unruly kids. My script involved a game of Monopoly which his family played as a harmless diversion. He kept tabs on them via an intercom, assumed their monopoly game was real and consequently bought up most of the Real Estate in Atlantic City. My script was turned down because of a possible lawsuit with Parker Brothers. The Dick Van Dyke script was considered very clever, but too political. I was a flop.

But I still had a little bit of Canada with me from my last trip. It was the book "Klee Wyck" by Emily Carr, the very book that got her the Governor General's medal and restarted her fading career as a painter. I set about trying to make a screenplay out of her frustrated artistic life.

Then came a phone call from a familiar voice from long ago. Norman Campbell calling me to ask permission to use the title song from our Anne musical. It seems that Wayne and Shuster had been commissioned to create a Variety show for the opening of the Charlottetown Confederation Center of the Arts.

This was a project that had started back in 1950 by an academic called Frank McKinnon, a professor of political science at the University of Calgary, but formerly of Prince of Wales College in Charlottetown. He was a witty man, the author of five books, winner of the Governor General's Literary Award for non-fiction. He instituted a competition for the design of the new center. There were forty seven entries from across Canada. The prize was won in 1962 by a young Greek architect. Dmitri Dimakopoulos. Frank McKinnon was pleased with the design but couldn't resist making a joke about it. He rearranged the classical poet Homer's famous quotation: "Beware of Greeks bearing gifts" into "Beware of gifts bearing Greeks"

The project might not have proceeded further without an insistent prodding of the Diefenbaker government by this same Frank McKinnon. He got them to cough up some development funds and the money was finally agreed to by all political parties three months after the architectural competition. Now what had been on paper could experience real dirt. The first sod was turned in February 1963 by Robert Stanfield, Premier of Nova Scotia (and the finest Prime Minister Canada never had). The cornerstone was laid by our very own Nobel prize winner and peace-monger deluxe Prime Minister Lester B. Pearson, in August of 1963.

The first actual theatrical presentation in the new theatre was the Dominion Drama Festival's week long competition in May of 1964. The official opening took place on October 6th. It was celebrating the centennial of the 1864 meeting of the Fathers of Confederation and Her Majesty Queen Elizabeth would be in attendance. The Queen and Prince Philip arrived in Charlottetown aboard the yacht Britannia, welcomed by Governor General George Vanier. Also present were the Prime Minister, the Premier of Prince Edward Island and the Mayor of Charlottetown.

The theatre had 1100 seats. The sound was amplified by suspended acoustical reflectors that Johnny Wayne and Frank Shuster called elephant diapers. The variety show had Lorne Greene as the Master of Ceremonies. Guest artists included Maureen Forrester, Glenn Gould and Oscar Peterson. Johnny and Frank wrote a special song for the occasion about the Fathers of Confederation. "They all sat down in Charlottetown and made themselves a land." I don't think that this great comedy team ever got enough credit for giving a jump start to our stage musical. To me, Wayne & Shuster along with Mavor Moore and Frank McKinnon are the true Fathers of Confederation Center.

Our little song about *Anne* would be the only piece of PEI in the whole show. I told Norm the song and the project had my blessing and promptly forgot about it.

"Anne of Green Gables never change, I like you just this way", was sung by Vancouver singer Diane Stapley to local performer Maida Rogerson, or perhaps it was the other way around, I wasn't there and I found out later that Norman was in Denmark shooting a film about a young ballet dancer for Walt Disney and Elaine was home, pregnant with their second child.

The next phone call I got regarding our long forgotten musical, was the morning following the special gala created by Wayne and Shuster, at an ungodly early hour in California. This time it was Mavor Moore, who after being the creator of Spring Thaw revues, the head of CBC TV and the founder of Toronto's St Lawrence Center for the Arts, not to mention THE true father of Canadian Musical Comedy, had been appointed as the first Artistic Director of the soon-to-exist Charlottetown Festival in the newly built Confederation Center of the Arts. A place that local skeptics had already referred to as "A darn good place to store all them pertaters."

Mavor was calling from Prince Edward Island. Our song had been sung with extra words that Elaine wrote for this special occasion *"young as the springtime, fresh as the rain, light as the laughter that brings me home again.*" The first words from Her Majesty's lips backstage were not how funny Johnny and Frank had been, (and believe me, thanks to their years of stage work in the Army Show, they were even funnier in the theater than they were on television,) but instead, "That's a rather pretty tune, where is the rest of the show?"

Mavor paused on this transcontinental phone call, waiting for my reply. Finally he resumed the conversation on his own "I don't know if you realize it buster, but that is a Royal Command." He implied that the next step would be to create a full fledged stage version of the television show we had done eight years ago, and it would open the second season of what was to be known as the Charlottetown Festival. My reply to Mavor was quite cryptic: "Get the rights, buster, and I'll start to work."

18 ON AGAIN ANNE

I decided not to wait for those rights but to make tentative moves toward a stage version of our orphan. Still living in California, I came back to Canada to do another television show. (The quickest way to get work in your own country seems to be, go away from it and be brought back as a guest star, even if you're not doing all that well abroad).

I had been divorced in 1960 and my ex-wife Gloria had remarried the author of the successful novel "In Praise of Older Women," Stephen Vizinczey. My daughters Martha and Mary were now teenagers and when I visited them in their Sherbourne Street home, they happened to be out, engaged in some kind of extra curricular school activity. However I was allowed to go to their bookcase and retrieve the original hard cover copy of *"Anne of Green Gables"* that I had read to them ten years before. I pulled it down from the shelf and got quite a shock. The interior of the book had been largely cut out, and inside there was all kinds of cigarette butts. I suppose I was relieved that they smelled of tobacco and not marijuana. It made me wonder if the novel I was planning to adapt for the stage would appeal to 1960's teenagers.

While waiting for the actual go-ahead from Mavor and his pursuit of the rights, I decided to bone up on the history of the novel and previous attempts to dramatize it.

Lucy Maud's first novel *"Anne of Green Gables"* was finished in 1905 and finally published in 1908 by L.C. Page of Boston. It was said that she got about a thousand dollars for her efforts and from what I can gather, that was about the last payment the publisher made to her. There were lawsuits to follow, especially after a film of the novel was made about 1920 starring Mary Miles Minter as Anne. I've never seen it, but there is a still picture showing the schoolhouse used in the film and there is an American flag flying above it. Apparently Miss Minter was involved in a scandal with William Desmond Taylor, the director of *"Anne of Green Gables"* silent movie. He was killed, perhaps murdered, and Mary Miles Minter was one of the suspects. This whole affair seemed to dampen interest in our pristine heroine Anne Shirley until 1935.

I did see the 1935 movie version, with sound of course. Anne was played by an actress called Dawn O'Day, (her real name was Dawn Paris.) The irony is that the owner of that name was so enamored of the part she played in that film that after its completion she had her name changed legally to Anne Shirley. Matthew was played by an old English actor, O.P. Heggie, and Marilla was Helen Westley. Gilbert was a well known juvenile actor, Tom Brown. There is no mention of a Mrs. Lynde but Mrs. Barry was played by Sara Haden and Diana was Gertrude Messinger. There was also a child actress part of the cast, her name Ann Miller (yeah, the dancer). I know all this trivia because I did a film called "The Best of Everything" with a young actress called Julie Payne, daughter of John Payne, (all those Alice Faye musicals) and the newly christened Anne Shirley.

Sam Mintz got the credit for writing the screenplay but I do remember that he drastically changed the basic plot. Instead of Anne and Gilbert having a feud throughout the entire story, Mr. Mintz decided that Anne and Gilbert were madly in love with each other from the beginning but they had to keep their love a secret from Matthew and Marilla who, untrue to the novel, had a feud with Gilbert's parents. In other words, the sneaky hack was stealing a plot from Shakespeare's Romeo and Juliet.

This had nothing to do with our rights to put the novel on stage. I left that up to Mavor Moore. It was April, just before Easter when he finally called to give me the go ahead.

"Congratulations Mavor. When do we open?"
"Middle of June"
"Holy Sh..!!!"
"Exactly. Get busy!!!"

19 ON THE PHONE AGAIN

Norman said the prospect of putting Anne on stage was like a big inhalation of breath. A chance to expand on a large space, something that had cabined, cribbed and confined us. No close-ups now, lots of stage space to do extra numbers we had never even thought of. There was no opening number in the TV show. It opened with a meeting in Rachel Lynde's house and the first lyric was caused by Matthew driving by in the buggy.

My memories of my parent's Sunday School experiences fueled me to write "Great Workers for the Cause." I remember my mother giving the biggest compliment to her female friends when she described them as great workers in the church. Meanwhile their teenage son Donald Hugh Harron was sniggering at the double—entendre names of my parents Bible Classes. My father belonged to the Hustlers and my mother was a Joy girl. This was at the Bathurst Street United Church where I was baptized, and in the Sexy Sixties shuttered briefly to reopen as The Red Light theatre. It has lately recovered its dignity as The Randolph Academy of Dramatic Art, where the graduating class did a wonderful production of "*"Anne of Green Gables""* a couple of years ago.

The long distance calls began anew with Norman and Elaine, this time between Toronto and Los Angeles. As fate would have it, I got busy in network television and we really wrote the stage version of Anne in two different countries. Sometimes the lyrics would come first and sometimes it was the music. We were all flying by the seat of our pants.

All of a sudden I was involved in show after show in Hollywood. I did "Twelve O'Clock High" twice inside a month, once as an American coward and then as an RAF Wing Commander leading an escape from a German prison camp. At one point it got so desperate that Norm flew out to L.A. while I was working on the second "Twelve O'Clock High." In between takes of the TV show, we worked on expanded dialogue scenes and lyrics for new songs. Sitting there in my RAF Wing Commander's uniform, I would stay with Norman for as long as I could before dashing back to the escape tunnel.

Norman confessed that he didn't really remember how he got the CBC to send him to Hollywood. All he knew is that he wouldn't have paid for it himself. He was so careful with his money that I remember us driving round and round Hollywood until he could find a free place to park and see a movie.

Back in Charlottetown, artistic director Mavor Moore came to our rescue with the lyrics for three of the best numbers in the show. First the gossip song "Did you hear, did you hear" involving the whole community where Josie Pye lies about Gilbert Blythe getting a concussion from Anne banging the slate on his head. Then the song "Open the Window" for the new female teacher, Miss Stacy, replacing the lecherous male teacher, Mr. Phillips, who gets a better paying job in the feed store. Finally, the heartfelt song expressed first by Matthew and later on by Marilla, two people who had difficulty revealing their feelings, "I Can't Find The Words."

This splendid output didn't surprise me at all. Mavor Moore was the true father of the Canadian Musical. First as the creator of Spring Thaw, he took the theme song he wrote for it "It's the Spring" and changed it to "Go to Hell" for his musical version of Voltaire's "Candide" called "The Best of All Possible Worlds." He also wrote a musical called "Sunshine Town" based on Stephen Leacock's "Sunshine Sketches of a Little Town," another musical based on the novel "Little Lord Fauntleroy," and then Charles Dickens's "A Christmas Carol." Oh yes…he also wrote an opera with Harry Somers based on the life of Louis Riel.

Coming up on his near-future horizon was the next big hit of the Charlottetown Festival. A story based on the 20th Century Fox musical, "Johnny Belinda" written by Mavor with a score based on Maritime folk music. But that was yet to come. In 1965 Mavor Moore was content to save our Canadian bacon and made it possible for us to open the show on time.

There was another person we felt forever thankful for and that was the original author. When we wrote the song that ends the school concert, "If it hadn't been for me" Norman, Elaine and I know that all this never would have happened "if it hadn't been for Lucy Maud."

20 CASTING ASPERSIONS ON MARILLA

Meanwhile Alan Lund was assembling a cast derived mostly from the show he was currently involved in and touring the country, "Spring Thaw '65." But to complete the cast he was poaching on the Wayne and Shuster Revue as well. The Festival consisted of a repeat of that Revue, plus a compilation of Stephen Leacock sketches made into a theatrical evening, "Laugh with Leacock," arranged by John Drainie who also played Leacock.

John had first played the Wit of Brewery Bay for me when I wrote a TV script based on the last chapter of the Sunshine Sketches novel. It was called "L'Envoi" and consisted of the author reminiscing about his old hometown of Orillia. John Drainie will always be Stephen Leacock for me. Except that he was equally memorable as our very first Matthew in the television version in 1956. The last item of that first season to open at the Confederation Center theater was our musical, so it had a pretty brief run.

The first Anne in our stage musical was a little gal from Texas, Jamie Ray. She was not in the Spring Thaw cast but was part of television's Tommy Hunter show. Don't ask me how she got from there to the stage of the Confederation Center but she filled the bill. Most of the rest of the cast seemed to come straight from the tour of Spring Thaw.

Anne's friend, Diana Barry, was played by Marilyn Stewart with a wonderfully sly wit. When Anne said tearfully that she might lose her friend to marriage in later years and blurted out "I just hate your husband," Marilyn's checking over her shoulder for the invisible spouse was a wonder to behold.

The sleazy teacher who necked at the back of the class with the prettiest girl, was played by Marilyn's beau and soon-to-be husband, Jack Duffy. He played the part like a riverboat gambler who expected to be caught cheating.

Gilbert Blythe was a tall dancer who reminded me of Ray Bolger, Dean Regan. His most vivid memory of that occasion was being held down by both Alan Lund and business manager Bob Dubberley while they cut his hair shorter. Wasn't this the swinging sixties?

The girl who slandered Anne with gossip, Josie Pye, was Gail Lepine, the part played later by Diane Nyland, who went on to become the Artistic Director of the Charlottetown Festival.

Mrs. Rachel Lynde, the gossip, was played by a senior English actress, Maud Whitmore, who is fondly remembered, many years after her passing, by an annual concert named in her honour.

The part of Matthew was a natural for Peter Mews. We had been together in several plays for the New Play Society, like the "Playboy of the Western World," Ibsen's "Ghosts," not to mention several early Spring Thaws. I was delighted to hear this.

I wasn't as pleased to hear that Barbara Hamilton would be playing Marilla. I admired her as a comic foil but wasn't sure that this would serve the gravity of the character of Marilla. Fortunately, my advice was ignored.

21 ABSENTEE AGAIN

I got another television job in L.A. that June and it prevented me from attending the world premiere of our musical. It was an episode of "The Fugitive" with David Jannsen. The part I played was that of a U.S. Army officer in charge of a nuclear installation and to save you the entire plot let's just say I let the Fugitive go.

The night *"Anne of Green Gables"* opened I was somewhere in the Mojave Desert trying to avoid scorpions beneath my feet. I went to my motel bed wondering how things went on stage in Charlottetown, not reckoning with the persistence of a Norman Campbell. He called me at an ungodly hour of the morning…it must have been around four a.m., (the time that Ingmar Bergman calls "The Hour of the Wolf," and he made a film with the same title.) but it was about eight a.m. Charlottetown time. Norman was born in California quite a while ago, but maybe he didn't realize that we were in a different time zone. Maybe he was just too excited. Believe me he certainly was excited. My composer and co-lyricist shouted into the phone "We got away with it! These Maritimers accepted our Upper Canadian version of their own story."

Then Norman went on to babble enthusiastically about Prince Edward Island. How he, Elaine and the kids had driven from Toronto, taken the ferry and tried its clam chowder. Elaine had first seen the Island back in 1944 as part of a Royal Canadian Air Force Women's Division basketball team. The game was in Summerside and they arrived by air. She wrote "flying low I saw this incredible place. It had shoals of turquoise and sand and a quilt of farms. It was paradise. We lost the game."

Elaine Leiterman from mine-scarred Northern Ontario never thought that some day she would be back to Paradise. Her description from the ferry in 1965 again reveals her talents as a lyricist. Here is her reaction "Suddenly we look out and there are shafts of low sunlight hitting the green grass, greener than I have ever seen, trees, neat houses, a fairy land. In my head I was hearing the orchestration of *"Anne of Green Gables."* Actually the orchestra they heard on opening night consisted of two pianos, a trumpet and a set of drums.

Norman walked into the theatre and thought "Fantastic, wonderful, big professional theatre, whoever designed it, did it for all time. We didn't know it was for us."

Almost as soon as he got to the Island he had to leave for London where he was, ironically enough, shooting a documentary on Wayne & Shuster for the TV program "Telescope." He was only away a week and came back the day before dress rehearsal.

With Elaine he went to that pre-dress rehearsal and shared the same reaction when Barbara Hamilton as Marilla sang Mavor Moore's lyrics "I Can't Find The Words." Lyricist Elaine best expressed their mutual feelings "I had never heard Barbara sing. She sang "The Words" and I was a total mess, tears rolling down my face. It was the most moving thing." Norman said "I knew that Alan had things going very, very well. We loved what we saw."

What they saw was a musical in which the title character spends approximately sixteen minutes off stage and two hours and five minutes on stage.

Jamie Ray told me she was so terrified on opening night that she temporarily blacked out during the opening scene with Matthew at the railway station. It wasn't so much that she lost consciousness, she just lost the ability to open her mouth and speak. She was saved by Peter Mews who tossed her a line that wasn't in any script, and completely uncharacteristic of the normally shy taciturn Matthew. Jamie says: "Peter Mews saved me that night."

Of the opening night, Norman claimed he couldn't remember anything. Elaine told him "Yes you can. You sat beside the critic Nathan Cohen." Norman does remember the opening night party with Bruno Gerussi and everybody boozing it up except the tee-total Campbells. There were skeptics at that party. Local sophisticates who felt that such an old fashioned story with an orphan, a spinster and a bachelor in the leading roles would never catch on in the Swinging Sixties. Chacun à son goût as they say in French. (This does not mean shakin' with the gout!)

Elaine remembers driving Mavor Moore home after opening night and getting totally lost on the Brighton Shore. Couldn't have been the booze with a tee-total Christian Scientist at the wheel, that's for sure.

22 THE CRITICS ON THE HEARTH

The reviews were yet to come. The first one was written by an eighteen year old cub reporter for the Charlottetown Guardian. Her name, Nancy White, and she bubbled over with praise for our venture. She bubbled so much about the musical *Anne of Green Gables* that the next year she was hired by the Charlottetown Festival to write all their publicity. Now, forty years later, she lives in Toronto and she is the lyricist for a musical sequel to our show called "Anne and Gilbert," which has definitely taken on a life of its own.

The second review of the 1965 opening night performance was written by the dean of Canadian drama critics, Nathan Cohen. I always called him good old reliable Nathan from the "Guys and Dolls" lyric, because he could generally be relied upon to pan the living daylight out of most shows. Recently two backstage crew members, Roddy Diamond and Rick Wilson, told me that they used to prowl antique stores so that they could present Nathan with a new cane when he came to review Charlottetown shows. I suspect that they might have given Nathan a cane with a sword in it, the better to slaughter us with.

Norman told me that Nathan arrived at the theatre that night as a genuine redneck. Literately. He had been out deep sea fishing and the back of him was the color of a cooked lobster. He sat beside Norman and Elaine, but flushed with the efforts of the afternoon, proceeded to fall asleep during a quiet moment in the first act. When Norman realized this (a snore is just a snore) he claims he gave the back of that red neck a poke. Nathan woke up, but it was very soon time to go out for intermission. Whatever he imbibed during that time, or perhaps the power of the sun on flesh, he fell asleep again during the second half. So essentially he didn't see our show. His review belied the fact. Actually it contained praises, fairly reserved praise but it ended with the catchy phrase "SOMETHING WONDERFUL IS HAPPENING IN CHARLOTTETOWN."

Catchy? It has been quoted by the Festival ever since.

23 SLINGS AND ARROWS

How to explain this change of heartlessness.

Let me try. Nathan Cohen is a Maritimer from Glace Bay, Nova Scoria. Maritimers are intensely loyal. When Nathan wrote a play for Dora Mavor Moore's New Play Society called "Blue is for Mourning," part one of a three play suite about a Cape Breton miner, it received a pasting from previously pasted-by-Nathan playwrights turned critics who were lying in wait for him. He had criticized Lister Sinclair's play "Man in a Blue Moon" as a radio snippet released on stage prematurely. Lister got to review Nathan's play and made the comment that Parts Two and Three, which were yet to appear, should be subject to mercy killing.

Suffice it to say that when our Anne appeared on stage in Toronto a couple of years later, Nathan got out his cane and did the expected slash job.

24 VARIETY'S SPICE AND DANNY'S KAYO

I finally got to see the show for myself in mid-July. By that time "*Anne*" had been pleasantly reviewed in Variety, the Bible of show business, by its resident drama critic Hobe Morrison. His assessment of our piece was that of a big city show-bizzy look at a little country kid but at least it was a pat on the back, even if a bit patronizing.

(I never forgot a Variety headline announcing that films about country folk were not generally box office in rural communities: HIX NIX STIX PIX).

But Hobe Morrison's review sparked some interest in L.A. L.A land. Janet Roberts, my MCA agent came up from New York and was encouraging. She told us we had a bid from Danny Kaye's Dinah Productions (pronounced Deena as in his version of the song i.e. Is there anyone feena in the state of Caroleena?) I was with Norm and Elaine when we actually got the offer on the phone from California. It came from a Canadian who worked for Danny Kaye's office. I will not mention his name because the offer was so insulting. It suggested that this Hollywood production company would do a film of our musical if it could get the score rewritten by someone with name value like…ohh…Andre Previn.

Norman's reply of "No Thank You" was measured, restrained and even polite. I would have spit all over the phone had I been on the line.

25 ANNE AT FIRST SIGHT

It was my first visit to Prince Edward Island. After California sunshine, the weather in Charlottetown seemed quite inhospitable and in the few days I spent there, I got myself a real summer cold. I felt quite miserable with my stuffed head but it didn't detract me that much from the enjoyment of seeing our musical on stage for the first time. Alan Lund had done a first rate job of keeping all things bright and beautiful, helped by John Fenwick at the podium who conducted his own wonderful arrangements.

The little Texas Anne, Jamie Ray, had big eyes like Joan Crawford and a big voice to match. In one performance during the season, where Marilla discovers Anne hiding under the covers in the bedroom scene, Barbara

Hamilton as Marilla was a bit too energetic and not only the covers were removed but so was the green-hair wig. It ended up behind the house on the backstage cement floor. Fortunately an alert stagehand saw this and threw the wig up into the bedroom again where it bounced on the floor in front of the horrified Marilla. Jamie Ray says by this time the audience was in high hysterics.

Peter Mews's Matthew was a delight when he came in the house from the barn having to scrape the uno-what before coming in the screen door. Best of all was when he tried to sneak upstairs to see the disgraced Anne after the tongue-lashing of Mrs. Lynde, he wore a pair of boots that squeaked on every step.

Liane Marshall did a fascinating double as a crotchety Mrs. Blewett and a radiant Miss Stacy. You wouldn't have recognized the clean scrubbed teacher from the slovenly slattern Mrs. Blewett.

But most of all I was delighted with the performance of Barbara Hamilton as Marilla. She maintained a kind of flinty, subtle humor that had completely escaped me in my interpretation of the character. Consequently I couldn't wait to go backstage and apologize to her for my goof in doubting her Marilla-ness.

Peter Mews

Barbara Hamilton

Charlottetown Festival Archives

She was pretty philosophical about it. Barbara had had so much praise already that she was magnanimous toward me. She invited me back to her rented house with the rest of the gang where we all partook of Barbara's favourite recipe…shipwreck.

This is a concoction that involves almost anything that is handy in the kitchen. Barb throws it all together into a working class bouillabaisse that feeds everyone. Her performance in Anne does the same thing.

Barbara shared a lovely old house on the island with Peter Mews and Dean Regan. To quote Dean: "Barb was head matron and often rifled our shorts out of us while we were still in bed, to do the morning laundry. I soon stopped wearing underwear to bed." Dean was the embodiment of the hippie sixties, with long hair, high boots and flowing robes with beads. He bought a zither from an antique store and he and Jack Duffy both bought puppies from their new island friends Warren and Darlene Hood. For transportation Dean had two options, a motorcycle and his horse, which he brought from Ontario and boarded with the Hoods. (Warren and Darlene, not a bunch of delinquents). Dean claims he would ride either mode of transportation around the Island, naked as a jaybird to the delight of the neighbours. No wonder he says "I loved the Island people and maintain friendships from forty years ago."

During his final season at Charlottetown he introduced Alan Lund to his eventual replacement as Gilbert Blythe, Jeff Hyslop, a young man from British Columbia, with the face of an angel, a natural dancer blessed with a beautiful singing voice. Dean had brought him along to accompany his niece for the summer and arranged an audition for him with Alan. Jeff not only took over the role a year later, but later on became the resident choreographer for our musical for a couple of seasons. He went on to star at the Stratford Festival, on Broadway and overseas in London's West End.

Dean Regan went on to create some successful musicals of his own; "Red Rock Diner" a show featuring swing music, somewhat different from the one Alan Lund created at Charlottetown called "Swing," and the well known production "A Closer Walk With Patsy Cline" which thrives today. Dean says much of the success he has had since those Charlottetown days he owes to the kindness and generosity of his mentor Alan Lund. He quotes "these were training days in my life and career. Alan brought out my natural ability to dance all forms with ease."

I have my own memories of Barbara Hamilton's generosity. I have been married to her twice, on television that is. After appearing as Charlie Farquharson's wife Valeda on our satire show for Global television, "SHhhhhhh...it's the News" Barbara talked me into celebrating International Women's Year by becoming a drag queen. Namely, I became Barbara's television wife, while she became my husband, in the embodiment of her own father complete with a bald pate and a walrus moustache. We became Charles and Valerie Rosedale, the town mice to Charlie Farquharson and Valeda's country mice, commenting on events in the news.

Years later when she passed away, I learned that she had left me six of her best dresses in her will. (By now, I'm the same size). As Valerie Rosedale, I still wear them with pride and gratitude to a warm wonderful woman who was unconditionally generous to me both on and off stage.

26 ENCORE ALREADY!

I was back in California and got a call from Mavor about the future. The board of the Charlottetown Festival decided our *"Anne of Green Gables"* musical would be done again the following season. This time the orchestra of two pianos, one trumpet and a set of drums would be augmented by...hold onto your hat...the Halifax symphony. In addition, Mavor wanted me to come and play the lead in "The Ottawa Man," his Canadian version of Gogol's "The Government Inspector." It was the part Danny Kaye had played in the film "The Inspector General." Maybe my future lay back in my own country! I shouted into the phone "YES, YES, YES!"

27 PRODIGAL RETURN

Later that month, after the Festival had closed down, I heard from Mavor Moore again. Alan Lund was so pleased with our *"Anne of Green Gables"* that he wanted to do another Canadian musical next season. I knew that Alan and his wife Blanche had starred in the Canadian Navy Show during the war, so I suggested that maybe we should try a musical version of Earle Birney's "Turvey," the war comedy I had adapted from his novel, and that Mavor had brought to stage in Toronto. He immediately agreed. He said he would contact Earle's agent, Mattie Molinaro, of the Canadian Speakers and Writers Service. I told Mavor that she was my agent too. She had been suggested to me by another of her clients, Lister Sinclair. I came on board when I did the first version of Earle's novel.

It was now October and the following May I would be coming to Canada and stay for the summer. I had made up my mind. I would leave California for good and come back to Canada to stay.

28 TURN ANOTHER TRICK?

I got back on the long distance phone again with the Campbells in Toronto. They had just come back from Prince Edward Island and they were already looking for a property to buy, something that looks like Green Gables, in case we ever do a film version, Norman said.

I told them about the offer of a second musical to pair on stage with our *"Anne of Green Gables"* and that I wanted both of them on board with me in the same capacity they had had before. I told them I would come to Toronto as often as I could before taking up permanent residence in the fall.

29 REMAKING A PLAY

Norman also wanted to make some changes in our *"Anne of Green Gables"* musical. He felt that the writers of American musicals get a longer rehearsal period, plus a several weeks run in out-of-town theatres to work on rewrites before they tackled Broadway. But our Charlottetown team had had not much more than a couple of weeks to get *"Anne of Green Gables"* up and running. At the same time they were dealing with three other shows on the same stage; "Wayne & Shuster," "Spring Thaw" and "Laugh with Leacock." Alan Lund was a miracle worker.

As for the future of our orphan, both Norman and Elaine agreed that we must keep the integrity of the original novel. In a sense we were the guardians of our little musical *Anne*. But we were also determined to improve on what we had already done. As it turns out, it took the three of us five years of changes to get our musical just the way we wanted it.

But we had to take the three-act play I had made from Earle Birney's World War II novel "Turvey" and fill it with music and lyrics. First thing I did was to ditch the three act formula and chop the action in half. Act One would end with Turvey getting his most fervent wish…being sent overseas. The work of writing lyrics started on the long distance phone between Toronto and Los Angeles.

I began to solicit work in Toronto so that I could come back to the Campbell living room and write lyrics with Norm and Elaine. To keep the wolf from the door, I contracted with CBC Radio to do a daily, but pre-recorded show, with a bubbly gal called Pat Paterson. It was called "Side by Side." Pat would select musical numbers and I would dig up spoken words items on any subject.

Also Charlie Farquharson was born again. I got Norman Campbell's Sable Island sweater and Norm Jewison's father's hat out of the mothballs. I did solo monologues on "The Tommy Ambrose Show "and" "The Jackie Rae Show." I was also hired by an old college pal, E. Ross Maclean, who got me a weekly gig on Canada's most popular TV show at that time "This Hour Has Seven Days." For the first time Charlie became political. I scanned Toronto newspapers for material. My first appearance on the show coincided with the Soviet Foreign Minister Andrei Gromyko being granted an audience with His Holiness the Pope. Charlie's take on this event was to comment "Yer Andy Gorwmickey was one of them Serviette Commonists, and you take yer averidge Pope he'd be morn likely a Roaming Cathlick, so how in the Sam Hill do yiz expeck fer to git a audience fer a thing like that?"

All that and writing another Canadian musical began to make this would-be Hollywood actor-writer feel All-Canadian again, especially back in the Campbell living room with Norm, Elaine and Puff the Magic Chow dog. I must add that in the fifty years of collaboration with Norman and Elaine, we never once had a quarrel. I attribute some of this to the Campbells adherence to their Christian Science faith, but mainly it was their own sunny natures. It gave them both boundless optimism, as they always presented such a unified disposition to enjoy the work of creation. It succeeded in reforming my own neurotic paranoia which I had inherited from my life in California. As a Hollywood actor, I had been taking amphetamines to lose weight, prescribed by a show-biz doctor who knew he was flouting the law. These pills made me high-strung, edgy and snarky. Norman hinted that I should get off the pills, forget about my weight and relax while Elaine brought me another muffin and a big cup of tea.

30 DOUBLE DUTIES

We took time out from our World War II Musical to rework a scene in *"Anne of Green Gables,"* the one where Matthew goes to the store to buy Anne the dress with puffed sleeves. Instead of a dialogue in prose, we decided to turn the whole situation into a musical number. We never got to complete it for another year.

Norman happened to be president of the Television Directors and Producers Association and they were holding meetings about the desirability of going on strike. There was a not too civil strife between CBC News and Public Affairs. At the center of it was the show I was a small part of, "This Hour Has Seven Days," conceived and directed by Elaine Campbell's brother Douglas Leiterman. It was the most popular television show on the CBC, a must-see for anyone in front of the box on Sunday night. It was rumoured that the news department was jealous of this public affairs rating success.

What has all this to do with writing a musical? Norman's continuous absence left Elaine to write lyrics which Norman would set to music when he had time. I had had hints of Elaine's ability with a lyric as far back as the television version of *Anne*, but because of our absent composer, I became impressed and highly dependent on Elaine Campbell's talent. By the time Norman got back to the project, "This Hour Has Seven Days" had been canceled and I had television work in California that would pay the rent. It wasn't till we gathered in the Confederation Center to hear the tunes Norman had matched to our lyrics that I was able to appreciate his amazing contribution.

Instead of what we had in the pit for the first season, two pianos, John Fenwick and Fen Watkin, with Ted Warburton on trumpet and Ray Reilly on drums (later to be chief timpanist for the Toronto Symphony), I was astounded with the sight of twenty six players from the Atlantic Symphony. In his own arrangements, John Fenwick paid no attention to Phil Nimmons's TV score. Norman gave the charts to John. The chords you hear are Norman Campbell's but the overall effect is pure Fenwick. John worked closely on Alan Lund's requirements for the dances; the egg and spoon race at the picnic is a musical highlight in the show.

That June of 1966, the cast, the Campbells and I heard for the first time the complete score of both musicals, *"Anne of Green Gables"* and "Turvey," using John Fenwick's arrangements for full orchestra. What a contribution John and the Atlantic Symphony made to our musical! Elaine said: "That's what Canadian theatre needs more of. Choreographers, composers, arrangers and directors feeling the music and knowing what's needed to happen to bring it all together."

31 BOTH SIDES NOW

While Alan Lund got "*Anne*" ready for it's second season, I was in rehearsals for Mavor Moore's "The Ottawa Man," set in pre-Confederation Canada, the Canadian rendition of Nicholai Gogol's classic farce "The Government Inspector." Mavor had summoned a first-rate Canadian cast, among them Eric House as the Mayor and Kate Reid as his wife. Their daughter was played by an unknown Charlottetown actress called Gracie Finley.

Alan Lund had used a few local actors the first year of *Anne*, for example all the young children in the school scene. The part of Mrs. Spencer, the lady who made the mistake of bringing Anne from the orphanage in Nova Scotia instead of the boy that Marilla and Matthew Cuthbert wanted, was played by Esther Pletch, (a name that could have been dreamed up by Lucy Maud herself.)

Gracie Finley had been a success in a play at the local drama festival. She seemed to me a natural to play Anne. I asked her if she could sing and she said she wasn't sure. I told her that perhaps she could take some vocal lessons. When she asked me why, I told her that to me she looked like an orphan, and that the sooner Anne was played by a local Charlottetown girl, the better.

A meaningful addition to the company was Diane Nyland, replacing Gail Lepine in the part of Josie Pye. She became a permanent fixture of the Festival, ending up eventually as choreographer and later on as artistic director. Diane also became part of the cast for the Centennial edition of "Spring Thaw '67" that I wrote. She played a pert saucy version of Laura Secord with lots of double entendre in her chocolate box.

We needed pretty girls like Diane in the cast of "Turvey." We also required good lookers who could play a couple of Piccadilly commandos, (whores de combat), in the number "We're Having a Couple of Tarts for Tea" as played by Marilyn Stuart and Judy Armstrong.

To uphold the religious end, I played the chaplain who had a double entendre sermon on chastity to deliver to the boys going overseas: "I suppose a lot of you chaps are family men and I don't need to tell you that a real family man now...he loves his wife and children and doesn't go chasing after...and...and all that... that entails. I say to you single men, who may have sweethearts waiting, I say unto you: for the backslider in heart shall be filled with his own ways, but a good man shall be satisfied from himself. As the poet says, I see you stand like greyhounds in your slips. Rahab is among us and Lilith….standing on street corners and beckoning with their hire, but remember lads, it isn't worth it. Take it from me."

32 TWO FANCY DIVAS

Charlottetown's second season opened with *"Anne of Green Gables"* and "The Ottawa Man" on successive nights. "Turvey" was to come later in the season

We had two great ladies of Canadian theatre on our roster. Kate Reid and Barbara Hamilton had been drama students together at the Royal Conservatory of Music and both had appeared in productions at Hart House theatre. They were old pals, but the sense of rivalry was always present

Barbara was back as Marilla in *Anne*, and Kate co-starred with me as the mayor's wife in Mavor's version of the Russian Farce, "The Ottawa Man."

Barbara was also in "Turvey" as Nurse "Stoney" Hart, a rather like the bullying female nurse in "One Flew Over the Cuckoo's Nest." She had a satirical number called "Angel of Mercy" which she belted out like a storm trooper: "*I'm a registered nurse, the best in my profession and I register my feelings with a bed-pan expression.*"

Kate, a trouper in her own right, wasn't in *"Anne of Green Gables"* but played an old drunk in "Turvey"'s scene in an old English pub. She wanted a song to go with her tipsiness.

I didn't know what to do about it but Norman did. He dreamed up an English pub tune called "*Buy a Drink for Old Muvver and She'll be a muvver to you.*" Norman and I wrote the lyrics to this song while I was performing in the "Ottawa Man," often clandestinely hidden under Kate Reid's petti-coats. (see photo in my biography "A Parent Contradiction" by my daughter Martha Harron). I would rush off stage, Norman would be there with pen and pad in hand, and we would add a line or two of lyrics until I had to go back on stage again: "*Boys be nice to your muvver, just think what she's been thru…Three Guiness, five Porter, a Double Double Gin and water, I can stand another if you can stand me to it. Let muvver be ruined by you!*"

These were lyrics about booze by two men who did not touch the stuff.

33 THE SHOW AFTER THE SHOW

That second season of the Charlottetown Festival will always be a highlight for me because of the camaraderie among the cast. Every night after the performance, whether *"Anne of Green Gables,"* "Turvey" or "Ottawa Man," we improvised an impromptu show where everybody did their party piece. Earle Birney was there with his poet friend, Al Purdy, and they both gave rousing renditions of their more comical works. Earle made wonderful clackety-clack sounds as he described a train journey across Canada. Al Purdy was hilarious in describing how he had a dump in the frigid regions of the high Arctic.

Jack MacAndrew was Alan Lund's right hand man. He made sure the show-after-the-show went on every night. By the second season, the cast members were writing crude parodies of the songs in our show, mostly of a sexual…nay, homosexual nature: "*we queerly requested a boy" "did you hear, did you hear Gilbert Blythe is turning queer"* etc. I remember doing a sketch with Diane Nyland, our Josie Pye on the mainstage, where I was Matthew and she played Anne in a short blackout in which I said, "Anne don't ever change" She replied " But Matthew, that's so unsanitary."

34   BACKSTAGE MANNERS

There was a nice tradition provided by the crew; special chairs for the Ladies of Avonlea to sit on while Anne and Diane performed what came to be known as the drunk scene. While waiting, one of the ladies, usually Marilla, would bring along cookies for the other ladies to munch on; and when a basket came down from the fly gallery, the extra cookies were put in it for the crew up above. On closing night the crew reciprocated by sending down for the ladies-in-waiting a bottle of champagne. Peter Mews as Matthew would not bother going back to his dressing room after he passed away in that rocking chair. Instead he would sit under the backstage stairs waiting for his curtain call. So stage crew chief Roddy Diamond took to leaving a tiny bottle of Scotch hanging just above Peter's head.

Other traditions began in those first seasons around the closing night performance.

There is one at the beginning of Act II when the performers hide behind the board fence waiting to perform "Where did the Summer go to" when they sign their names and leave messages about what a good time they had this summer. Heidi Ford (Diana) left her gum there. It's still there, completely shellacked over.

Also in the classroom scene, when the pupils of Avonlea school were ordered to get on with the work they didn't do yesterday, while their teacher necked with the prettiest pupil in the back row, some of them expressed themselves on their slates in a more adult way e.g. one slate said "I wanna make love to you in a blueberry field."

One closing night gesture that was never repeated to my knowledge, was played by Dean Regan (Gilbert) on his old Spring Thaw pal, Marilyn Stuart. He spiked her raspberry cordial bottle with Canadian Club and the audience experienced a genuinely tipsy Diana that night. I doubt it has happened since, although the crew still tend to play little jokes.

Another closing night incident not to be repeated occurred when the actor playing Moody Spurgeon Macpherson, who is soaking a prune for recess, is told to get rid of it by the teacher Mr. Phillips. As the text requires, Moody deposits it in the teacher's hand. This Mr. Phillips (who shall remain nameless) flung the prune pit across the stage and instructed Moody to get on his hands and knees and go fetch it.

35 CA-NA-DA!

During its third season, our musical started to receive offers of a cross-Canada Tour. *"Anne of Green Gables"* on the road was to start as soon as the Charlottetown season ended, including a three week engagement at Montreal's Worlds Fair, Expo 67.

Centennial Year 1967 is generally thought of as our nation's finest hour. It certainly seemed that way to me. I arrived from the United States to find that Canada had three things that America didn't have: a pension plan for seniors, a public health care system and a brand new flag. At one time the Pearson government was going to choose a flag with three maple leaves on it, but decided to go with the single leaf design. Some people thought it looked like the logo of a new gas station. I vividly remember Marilyn Stuart, the first Diana of the Charlottetown Festival, appearing in "Spring Thaw '66" at the Royal Alexandra Theatre, seemingly naked except for a single Maple Leaf over her pubic area, and with her hands over her breasts as she said rather shyly "I liked it better when there was three of them."

"Anne of Green Gables" at Expo was part of a national tour. According to Gracie Finley "Pierre Trudeau was a fan and never missed sending me an opening night bouquet."

At the same time I was doing a cross-country tour for General Motors advertising their new car models. When our paths crossed in Winnipeg I was able to see for myself that the show was indeed in good hands.

"Anne of Green Gables" also hit the road west to Calgary, Edmonton and Vancouver. When *Anne* was in Toronto at the Royal Alex Theatre, Bill Freedman, a Canadian producer based in London, UK, brought over English theater magnate Ian Albery to have a look. They both agreed that *Anne* had definite West End potential.

I'm glad they didn't see one particular performance at the Alex when Jamie Ray as Anne felt too sick to go on. But the stage management told Jamie that she was fine to go on as long as she could speak. Jamie went on, devastated and embarrassed by the fact that

Charlottetown Festival Archives

Gracie & Pierre Trudeau

she couldn't really sing. Carol Ann Clouston, the understudy, was available and by the third scene Carol Ann was on stage and Jamie cried all the way home in the taxi. Today Jamie is lead soloist in a church choir and has recently given a solo concert. She still has nightmares about that particular night at the Royal Alec. I didn t see Carol Ann's performance but it must have been full of delicious humor because she is the daughter of one of my favorite Newfoundland wits, Al Clouston.

I was thrilled that a local boy had enough faith to bring our show to London. Bill Freedman was a Toronto theatre entrepreneur who married his childhood sweetheart, Toby Robins. Toby who started with our New Play Society at the age of sixteen, rose to fame on weekly television as the sole female questioner on Front Page Challenge. Her most frequent query to a mystery guest was "Are you political in any way?" Eventually Bill and Toby moved to London but not before Bill had made his mark in Toronto as an imaginative theater showman. When he brought the English musical "Salad Days" to Toronto's Crest Theatre, he advertized the show by handing out free salads to curious pedestrians on street corners.

Bill planned the London opening of *"Anne of Green Gables"* to take place two years later in 1969. He was as good as his word. We needed to establish our right to produce the musical abroad so no one else could create a show by the same name but with different script and music. There were more than twenty one performances at the Royal Alex in 1967 which qualified *Anne* as a first class venue, so through the Dramatists Guild of New York theaters we were able to establish international rights to our musical. *Anne* had legally arrived on the world stage.

Since then we have heard of about at least five attempts in various parts of the United States to musicalize the novel. Did the Dramatists League grant them Grand Rights too? I just don't know. Because the novel is in public domain in the United States would-be playwrights think our musical is too. No, not till fifty years after I've been put six feet under.

36 NORMAN FOR EXPORT

The same international attention was happening to our composer Norm Campbell. He had established a reputation as CBC TV's most versatile director, staging comedies, dramas, ballets, Gilbert & Sullivan opera, Broadway musical "Pippin," and Stratford Festival productions of the classics. Occasionally he would take what he called month-long coffee breaks from the CBC. Said Norm ironically "I don't think they knew I was gone."

Norman Lear got him to guest-direct an episode of "All in the Family." After he got finished, their Norman offered our Norman to do a whole season, bunk in with the Bunkers. But our Norman had to come back to Canada and film a ballet with Karen Kain and somebody called Rudoph Nureyev.

Our Norm soon returned State side to do some "Mary Tyler Moore Shows," plus an award winning special with Diana Ross, in which she impersonated great stars like Billie Holiday, Ma Rainey, Bessie Smith, and a rousing presentation of the saucy number from "A Chorus Line," T. and A. (shorthand for Tits and Ass). His efforts won him an Emmy, but he was too busy with Canadian television at the time to accept in person, so he sent a CBC executive instead.

Norman also did television specials in London, England, and a Disney film in Copenhagen. But he always came back to us in Canada and despite a lack of pension (he was always a freelance you see) he continued to be loyal to the CBC. He said "it provided me with forty seven years of training. I'm also glad to come back to a country where life is more even than the ups and downs of American showbiz."

Norm had dual citizenship, Canadian and American, because he was born in California. He moved to Vancouver with his parents at the age of seven. He wrote his first song at that age. It broke all the rules. I can only provide you with the lyrics, and they are worth preserving.

> *ROLLING HOME, ROLLING HOME*
> *WHILE THE MOON IS SHINING*
> *ROLLING HOME, ROLLING HOME*
> *ALL OF US AND TARZAN.*

The melody that accompanies the words is pretty good too, even if it comes to an abrupt end.

37 AMAZING GRACIE

Gracie & Don
"Grateful author congratulates local girl

The local Charlottetown girl, Gracie Finley, had buckled down and taken those music lessons I suggested in 1966. She became the 1968 Anne and continued for seven years until the season of 1974.

That is when she got married to a young man with the improbable name of Barry Stickings and moved away to England, saving us the necessity of advertising Gracie Stickings as Anne. Actually her official name and address is Gracie Finley-Stickings, Willots Farm, Studridge Lane, Speen, Princes Riseborough, Buckinghamshire. UK.

In 1984, she came back from

England with two kids in tow, resuming her Charlottetown role of Anne for the next two seasons, looking exactly the same as she had in 1968. When we celebrated the 40th anniversary of Anne in the summer of 2004, the affair was co-hosted by Gracie and the first Charlottetown Festival Anne, Jamie Ray.

In November 2007, while I was in Charlottetown researching this book I was told that sadly I had just missed Gracie. She comes back to the Island from England quite often. Mrs. Stickings and husband Barry have got themselves a summer place on a point near Cavendish. (Could that be the Stickings Point?) In Gracie words: "*Anne* has been a major part of my life. Such joy and laughter. It was a magic place. *Anne* was special."

Our Gilbert that season was an amazing young dancer, Jeff Hyslop, who turned the second act "Shoe Dance," so called because most of it is performed in bare feet, into a tour de force by executing a complete 360 degree flip in the air.) He and Gracie made a wonderful pair as Anne and Gilbert, and I kept hoping that perhaps they would go on to perform in London.

Jeff later dazzled Stratford theatergoers along with another Charlottetown alumnus, Brent Carver, who played Hamlet in Cliff Jones's musical version of Shakespeare's greatest tragedy "Kronborg 1564," before going on to play the non-musical Hamlet at Stratford. While there, Jeff and Brent co-starred in Gilbert and Sullivan's "Pirates of Penzance." Both went on to star in the award winning musical "Kiss of the Spider Woman." Brent performed on the Broadway stage, where he got his well-deserved Tony Award. Jeff played in London's West End where I saw him give a great performance alongside Bebe Neuwrirth, that wonderful brunette from the TV Series "Cheers," who played Kelsey Grammer's icily superior wife.

At present, Jeff is producing summer theater in Campbell River on Vancouver Island where he does two shows a season. One is a play by Shakespeare, and the other is the same play with an original musical score added. Last year the company did an updated version of one of his plays set against the B.C. rain forest. When I asked musical director/composer/arranger David Warrack which play of the Bard's he and Jeff had musicalized, he replied: "A Midsummer Night's Wet Dream."

38 ONWARD AND UPWARD WITH THE ARTS

During the fourth Charlottetown season in 1968 the Campbells and I got back to work. Norman, Elaine and I started getting Anne ready for her West

End debut. We had managed to musicalize the scene where Matthew visits Blair store to buy the puffed sleeve dress for Anne. Instead of mere dialogue Matthew could now express all his puff-puff hesitation in a song.

We then decided to add a musical number where the scholarship rivals Anne and Gilbert Blythe confront each other. Elaine felt we should give Anne and Gilbert a chance to show their scholastic rivalry in a duet on an empty stage. This resulted in "I'll Show Him" which finally nailed the inevitable confrontation. Our show kept getting longer and longer. Alan Lund would discreetly remove some of the dialogue during the run of the season, but the show never shortened because he would simply add more choreography. After forty-four years this undercover battle still goes on between librettist and choreographer.

Artistic Director Mavor Moore never cut any of our dialogue. He was too busy creating it for himself in that 1968 season. To match our *"Anne of Green Gables"* he had two musicals on his stage: "Sunshine Sketches of a Little Town" and "Johnny Belinda."

The first was the Stephen Leacock novel that I had worked on the first season of CBC television. Mavor brightened things up even more with turn of the twentieth century period tunes to his lyrics.

It's interesting how some of the great musicals are set in the period 1900-1910. Think of Oklahoma, Carousel, My Fair Lady, Mary Poppins, Music Man...and...oh yes...dare I say...*"Anne of Green Gables"*?

The second Mavor musical that season was a real surprise. "Johnny Belinda" had been a successful 1940's film starring Jane Wyman (Miz Ronnie Reagan-that-was) as Belinda, a Nova Scotian deaf mute who is raped and produces a baby she calls Johnny. Mavor took some Maritime folk tunes, added his own song writing talent, and produced the second most produced musical in the history of the Charlottetown Festival. There are rumours that it will soon grace its stage again. Add a home grown production of the British comic classic revue "Beyond the Fringe" with Canadian comics like Don Cullen and Barry Boldaro performing it and our local girl Gracie as Anne, 1968 was a banner year.

39 LONDON CALLING

I never saw much of the 1969 Charlottetown Festival, neither did the Campbells. Norman was busy filming a television series with Liberace in

London at the same time as we were heavily involved in the West End presentation of our musical at the Albery Theatre in St. Martin's Lane.

Alan Lund was on board, thank the Lord, and so was John Fenwick as musical director. Alan had worked for Bill Freedman in London before in an English revue at the Arts Theater Club. Also Bill Freedman imported Barbara Hamilton as Marilla. Norman, Elaine and I were hoping that Bill might transport our Charlottetown heroine Gracie Finley in the title role, but Bill had his eyes on another rising star of English television, Polly James. She was presently starring in an English panto on the south coast and Bill was willing to pay my air fare to go over and check her out. I did.

Left London on one of those comfy English trains that serve hot tea and fruitcake in the dining car, and I ended up somewhere in Cornwall at a fairly dingy repertory theatre. Polly James was playing a character part, a weirdo not remotely like our Anne. It was when I went backstage to meet her that I realized she had the same quality I saw in Gracie Finley. She looked like an orphan. I trusted my instincts and told Freedman to go ahead and cast her.

It was then that he sprang a surprise on me. Instead of Peter Mews, who had created the role, and in my humble opinion set the benchmark for all time, Bill Freedman asked me to play the role of Matthew. I was stunned. My immediate reaction to his offer was "Do you think I want to ruin our show by putting Charlie Farquharson in there?"

The real reason was that I wasn't too sure of my ability to stay on key in the musical numbers. I had done a musical only once before, during my 1953-4 season with the Bristol Old Vic. It was called "The Merry Gentleman" and written by the team that later wrote "Salad Days," Julian Slade and Dorothy Reynolds. "The Merry Gentleman" was Santa Claus, or as the English call him Saint Nicholas, and played and sung extremely well by Douglas Campbell of Stratford-On-Tario fame. I was the juvenile lead opposite Jane Wenham, at the time the wife of Albert Finney. Jane was an established singer and the cast was augmented by two young singers from the West of England Light Opera Company, Joan Plowright, now Lady Olivier, and the actress who plays Hyacinth Bucket on the hit British TV sitcom, "Keeping Up Appearances," what's her name?…oh yes, Patricia Routledge.

Names. Names I have such trouble trying to remember them in my old age!

When I turned seventy, I asked Robertson Davies what was it like to be eighty. He replied in his deep voice which sounded like a bumble-bee in a jug "frequent urination and inability to remember names." I have inherited both frailties.

But with all that vocal talent on board in Bristol, I felt distinctly over-whelmed when I had to sing the duet "I'll Always Be in Love With You" with Jane Wenham, and more than a shred of panic when I had to sing solo "There's Only One, Only One Father Christmas." I think the English were too polite to tell me I was not cutting it.

For that reason I turned down the role of Matthew. I suggested Peter Mews but Bill Freedman felt Barbara Hamilton was enough Canadian con-tent in the leading roles. He suggested instead an American comic actor, Hiram Sherman, better known as Chubby, for obvious reasons.

I agreed immediately. I had spend two seasons at the American Shakespeare Festival in Stratford, Connecticut with Chubby Sherman where he played a twinkly Touchstone in "As You Like It" and a sly Pandarus in "Troilus and Cressida." I had never seen him in a contemporary play but he had just scored an enormous Broadway success portraying the humor colum-nist Art Buchwald of the New York Herald Tribune, in a stage collection of his columns written during his years in Paris. But beneath this sophistication I knew there was a farm boy who appreciated rural values. The deal was set. No Charlie Farquharson for Marilla. I breathed easier.

The rest of the cast were English, except for three actors. Two came from our Charlottetown company. Bob Ainslie who had played Moody Macpherson was chosen for Gilbert and Susan Anderson repeated her role of Diana Barry. The part of Miss Stacy was given to an American now liv-ing in London, (I wish I could remember her last name...Pat?...) She was very affable to work with and I cannot honestly say that this production was able to stand pat.

40 WE SNEAK INTO TOWN

There was no advance publicity for the show during rehearsals. Bill Freedman didn't want any. He had always wanted to bring a Canadian show to London but he didn't want the press to know in advance that it was from Canada. He felt the British critics would be anti-colonial.

He also wanted some drastic changes to some of our lyrics. "Bosom Friends" and "Open the Window" had to be out the window. Why you may ask? Because the American musical "Auntie Mame" was headed for London

Heidi Ford & Jennifer Toulmin
"Kindred Spirits"

soon after we opened and two of the hit songs were "Bosom Buddies and "Open a New Window."

Norman was so busy directing his TV series with Liberace for CBS that he only heard about our plight on the set. Liberace must have been listening too. The very next day there was a heavy knock knock at the door of Norman and Elaine's apartment in Hampstead. A burly delivery man said to Elaine "Missus Camel?…we got a pie-anner ere from Mister Libber-ace"!

Norman called me where I was in rehearsal at the Albery theatre and told me to get over to Hampstead quick. Evidently Liberace couldn't imagine his director Norman Campbell composing for a London opening without a piano. On my way there it was exciting to see posters of a dancing Anne in the tube station. It was a full color drawing that we have been happy to use ever since.

In eighteen minutes Norman, Elaine and I wrote a song to replace Bosom Friends called "Kindred Spirits" and it's been in the show ever since.

Once a year at the annual Sunday night performance in honour of the first Mrs. Lynde, Maud Whitmore, the show closed with Norman conducting the entire cast of performers in Bosom Friends. After we lost Norman in 2004, the conductor replacing him for that event was Norman's teenage grandson Jamie. His grandpa would have been proud.

To get back to the Campbell's flat in Hampstead, instead of "Open the Windows," we decided to merely change the title to the last line of the lyrics, "Learn Everything." To make sure the English theatre audiences knew where our show came from, Norman started playing an original march which was used in the school concert entitled "Prince Edward Island, the Heart of the World" It's still in the show.

Another song from Norman and Elaine that was created in their London apartment, was called "When the Heartbreak is Over." This was to mark Anne's reaction to Matthew' death. But we decided that when Anne sees Marilla grieving over Matthew's chair and a reprise of "I Can't Find the Words," Anne rises above her own grief to comfort Marilla. The song "When the Heartbreak is Over" was used later when the three of us created "The Wonder Of It All," the musical about the life of our Canadian painter Emily Carr.

We made one last change in the score. Chubby Sherman didn't feel he could do justice to the song "I Can't Find the Words" when he heard the magnificent way Barbara Hamilton did it. So we wrote him a more up-tempo number called "When I Say my Say." It's still on the CBS recording of the London production. I'm thinking of using it when we do the film of our musical. I envision Matthew working out his frustration of non-communication by telling his troubles to the various animals in the barn.

41 A FRIEND NEXT DOOR

During *Anne* rehearsals we learned that Barbara Hamilton's buddy and friendly rival Kate Reid was opening in a play a few rods down St Martin's Lane at the Duke of York's Theatre. It was an English play, (I can't remember the name) and at any rate it didn't last long, but it allowed the two great ladies of Canadian theater to get together and explore London between rehearsals. One of their expeditions ended badly when Barbara stepped off one of those London trains on the wrong foot, and ended up you-know-what over tea kettle. The foot wasn't damaged but the fall did something to Barbara's taste buds. From then on she could never taste any flavor in her food. This disaster happened to one of the great hostess-entertainer cooks of all time. Remember she was the inventor of "Shipwreck." Despite her lack of taste, strictly culinary of course, Barbara continued to be the hostess with the mostest, entertaining and feeding every stranded theater orphan at Christmastime in her Toronto home.

42 OPEN COLD, END UP HOT AND BOTHERED

Opening night in London found me in a strange mood. I should have been deliriously happy with my two teenage daughters beside me. I hadn't seen them for far too long, now that they were residing with their mother and step-father in Colherne Court, in the same apartment complex that also housed a young lady resident who would later be known as Princess Diana.

I think the main reason for my disquiet was having finally seen the set for our English production. It was by Henry Bardon, a distinguished designer of sets for operas. He was Austrian-born and his version of the Green Gables house looked more to me like a Swiss Chalet, (but I was too chicken to tell him so.)

So I entered the Albery Theatre that evening with an air of disquiet, not alleviated by the proceedings I saw on stage. There was nothing wrong with any of the performances. It just didn't feel like home. Norman and Elaine seemed ecstatic about our play and it's reception. I attended the after-theatre party at London's most famous show-biz restaurant, The Ivy. I was so out of place with my pessimism that I excused myself to Norman and Elaine and took a cab back to my hotel with instructions that no one was to disturb me. So much for that. Again it was at a very early hour of the morning that my hotel phone rang and a very excited Norman Campbell told me "we have a hit."

All nine London reviewers praised the innocence and freshness of our show. My instincts were again totally wrong, as they had been when we opened "Spring Thaw" at the Royal Alex in 1967. Again I had insisted that no one phone me about the reviews.

Harold Hobson of the Sunday Times declared that "it was an evening when it was good to be alive and in the theatre." He gave a lot of credit to our composer, although he penned his name as Norman Camp. Our Campbell fella didn't get upset. He was just thrilled to be recognized as a theatre composer instead of the TV guy who writes a few songs on the side.

Some weeks later, the British magazine Plays and Players published its list of awards for the 1969-70 season. *Anne of Green Gables* won it for Best Musical (sorry "Auntie Mame"). Polly James, Barbara Hamilton and Hiram Sherman all won Best Performance Awards. An extra award was for the only ballad in our show "Wond'rin" winning the prize for best single recording.

As Anne herself would say "It gave me great satisfaction."

This is what David Glyn-Jones remembers from attending the London Production. "In 1969 I took my two small boys to the UK to meet their grandparents (their mother had died some years earlier). My cousin was stage managing a show on the Strand and arranged tickets for us to see *Anne*. We took with us a very mod, very mini skirted daughter of upper class friends. The show was great and brought home closer for a little while. Best though was when I learned that the very mod young lady on my right was moved by Matthew's death and the succeeding scene of Marilla's mourning. There was hope for the future in her reaction.

Naturally I never expected, a quarter of a century later, to be playing Matthew myself in Charlottetown, and audibly producing the same reactions. I passed a Kleenex to my guest in London and should have immediately invested in the company that made them. Shows what a great part can do."

43 ABBEY NOT TOO SHABBY

We recorded the entire score for CBS records at the Abbey Road studios, made famous by the snapshot of the four Beatles walking across that road to record their Abbey Road album.

That was my last day in London and I wrote the liner notes for the album in a taxi on the way to Heathrow Airport.

I was on my way to Nashville Tennessee to start a CBS summer series called "Hee-Haw." This was the summer replacement for the "Smothers Brothers" show which had been canceled by the network because the Brothers and their young writers like Steve Martin and David Steinberg had been all too prescient about the Vietnam war.

The producers and creators of "Hee-Haw" were two U.S. based Torontonians, Frank Peppiatt and John Aylesworth, who had talked CBS into a country music-corn-comedy series on the basis of the title alone. To their credit they had already done a "Sonny & Cher" series, Judy Garland and Frank Sinatra specials.

To get some Canadian content into the show, Frank & John had asked Gordie Tapp and I to join the cast. I told them I couldn't possibly be there until after the London premiere of *Anne*. They agreed and I joined the show on its last day to record thirteen Charlie Farquharson's monologues I had written in London. The whole thing took me one hour and I headed back home to Toronto feeling like a Northern Carpetbagger from the Civil War.

In contrast to the ecstatic reviews from London, the reception of "Hee Haw" by the U.S. press was in dire contrast. The New York Times wrote that "Hee Haw" was the only summer replacement in TV history that required a summer replacement." Even worse was the review by Patrick Scott, jazz critic of the Toronto Daily Star. He wrote: "If you watch this show you do not deserve to own a television set."

H.I. Mencken once wrote "Nobody ever went broke underestimating the intelligence of the American people. "Laugh-In" a critic's darling, lasted three years and it was a much cleverer show, made up of the same twenty second comic blackouts as "Hee Haw." We used to call our show "Sesame Street for Grownups." "Hee Haw" lasted twenty five years. So much for critic's choice. Go figure.

I have a feeling that the name on my gravestone will be "Charlie

Farquharson, fifty five years old, born in Spring Thaw in 1952. It was a four minute delivery" while our *"Anne of Green Gables"* is only forty four years old.

Of course in this year of 2008, Anne is a centenarian and eagerly awaiting her letter of congratulation from Her Majesty Queen Elizabeth.

44 POSTLUDE

Despite its rave reviews and many awards, our *"Anne of Green Gables"* had a London run of just nine months. If Bill Freedman had been able to commandeer the charabancs (buses filled with theatergoers) to come to London we might had been there for years.

Turned out that the BBC was a fan of what we had done, and they whipped up a TV mini-series of the book (no musical numbers) starring Barbara Hamilton as Marilla and Bernie Braden's daughter Kim as Anne. I never got to see it. Barbara felt it came off frightfully English.

45 SWEDISH SURPRISE

It was after Norman, Elaine and I were back in Canada that we received the news that a theatre in Göteburg was interested in doing a Swedish language production of our musical. It was called "Anne Grönkulla" but none of us was able to take the time to get over there to see it. Norman was up to his ears in all kinds of network television and Elaine was having more babies. I was busy writing a film script for Bill Freedman who had touted me to a Hollywood producer after he had seen our show in London. The film producer was skeptical that the man who adapted the book of *"Anne of Green Gables"* could write a sex comedy about Washington during World War II. So I was passed over on that assignment.

To show Bill Freedman what I could do, I whipped up a theme that was as far from Lucy Maud's *"Anne of Green Gables"* as possible. It was about an eighteen year old boy whose mother died at birth and was raised by his grandmother, the only person who had ever shown him love. When the grandmother dies, the boy's father brings a sleazy common-law stepmother into the home and the boy runs off to the city and makes a living herding shopping carts in a super-market. One day he helps out a seventy year old woman and falls hopelessly in love with her. The script was called "Once." It opened with the boy burying the old lady in her backyard, having expired of a heart attack after reluctantly consenting to have sex with the boy. The young man surmises wrongly that once you have sex with somebody, they die.

Different from *'Anne of Green Gables'*? Well I should say.

I had a point to prove with Hollywood. Hal Ashby, who wrote the highly successful film "Harold and Maude" about a boy who falls in love with an 80 year old woman, told Norm Jewison that my script was more believable.

Anyway the script was ultimately done in a ninety minute version for CBC television directed by Gordon Pinsent and starring his wife Charmion King, along with a young unknown actor, Leslie Toth, who got an ACTRA Award for his TV debut. The only connection with our musical is that later Gordon Pinsent played a superb Matthew to Barbara Hamilton's Marilla in a special Alan Lund production of *'Anne of Green Gables'* at Toronto's Elgin Theatre. Gordon won an Award for it. Barbara didn't, even though she gave her usual brilliant performance. I would have loved to have been in the dressing room to hear her reaction. On second thought, no, I wouldn't. I prefer a peaceful existence.

46 OSAKA ANNE

Speaking of Barbara, she was able to finish up her BBC non-musical TV series of the Anne novel in time to come back to Canada and set off for the 1970 World's Fair in Osaka, Japan. This was before the regular summer season at Charlottetown, which consisted of the sixth season of "Anne," followed by a new musical version of Charlotte Bronte's "Jane Eyre," written by a couple of Englishmen, plus a revival of our 1966 musical "Turvey."

One of the perils of adaptation is when the original author is still alive. Earle Birney was demanding changes from the 1966 version.

"Gracie F. and Doug C. at Osaka '70"

Charlottetown Festival Archives

Faithful to his original novel we used euphemisms instead of four letter words. Earle felt the time had come to call a spade an effing shovel. He also felt our view of war was too warm and comfy. He wanted some of the horror to creep into our comedy. As I set out for Tokyo, I knew I would be too preoccupied to see much of Japan.

The plane took us to Japan in two jumps, Toronto to Vancouver, stay overnight, and then on to Japan. In Vancouver we were joined by some star performers bound for Expo 70, members of the RCMP musical ride. They were a jolly bunch especially when the drinks flowed freely. We figured their horses were tee-total and would keep them on the straight and narrow.

Gracie Finley remembers the flight over as one long party between the *"Anne of Green Gables"* cast and the musical riders who drank and drank. She found three empty seats and snuggled into the one by the window and was just about to fall asleep when a mountie sat in the aisle seat, grinned, said something resembling, "nishe party," and promptly collapsed in a bit of a stupor with his head on her lap. She couldn't budge him. Dougie Chamberlain (Mr. Phillips) found her being squashed and rescued her.

Roddy Diamond, our crew chief, says our Air Canada pilot took his time finding both the city of Tokyo and the airport. Roddy claims that you can't blame the pilot, because Japan is really one continuous city. But he did land the wrong way on the runway and deplaning passengers had to duck under the plane's wing to disembark. Gracie says "I don't remember any of that."

Why were we going to Japan with our Prince Edward Island show?

Because the Japanese felt about "Akage No An" (Red Haired Anne) the way German scholars felt about Shakespeare's Hamlet; that it was part of their culture, and they were just lending it to us. A translation by Marura Oka had appeared just before World War II and was taught in Japanese schools, despite Pearl Harbor.

Marura Oka's granddaughters Mia and Eri met with Lucy Maud's granddaughter Kate Butler at Japan's most recent World Expo in 2005. That was when Director Duncan MacIntosh took Jennifer Toulmin to World Expo 2005 to represent our *"Anne of Green Gables."* The issue of the male name came up in a conversation between Princess Takamado of the Royal House and Mr. Toyota himself, whatever his real name was. The meeting took place in Ngoya, the home of Toyota's hybrid cars. Mr. Toyota (who happens to be a fitness buff) raised the fact that because in Japan An was a boy's name, he thought our Anne would be a boy. The Princess who speaks flawless English because she was educated at Queen's University in Kingston Ontario, said sweetly: "So did the Cuthberts."

I think the real reason Anne is such a heroine to many Japanese women is because she never took any crap from the boys, and instead bopped one over the head with a slate. In 1970 we were told that the Japanese Crown Princess was coming to our opening performance without the Crown Prince. So there. One up for Women's Rib!

Jennifer Toulmin had met Princess Takamado previously in Charlottetown at the opening night of *"Anne of Green Gables"* in 2004. Because she played a genuine Canadian heroine, Jennifer was chosen, along with five other Canadians, to represent Canada at World Expo in 2005. During her visit Jennifer signed over 1000 autographs for Japanese fans who had flown to Charlottetown to see her play Anne in 2002, she was already known in Japan for playing Anne, because her face was on a collectors Expo-type baseball-type card and there was even a nation-wide contest to have a PEI lobster dinner with Jennifer-Anne!

47 TOKYO SHOWBIZ

Before going on to Osaka on a train that was supposed to travel at 300 miles per hour, we had a few days in Tokyo. Barbara Hamilton was anxious to see some Japanese Theatre. I had seen Kabuki productions in New York but the show that intrigued me was the all-girl Takashimiya Theatre. That theatre was later shown in the movie "Sayonara" with Marlon Brando, an American officer who falls in love with Hana-ogi a theatrical performer played by Kiiko Taka.

Barbara Hamilton was anxious to see it too. So we set off together in a cab.

Tokyo was the most confusing place I'd ever been in. Barbara insisted on using her newfound knowledge of Japanese. It consisted of two words, Waki= right and Miki= left. She kept giving the taxi driver wacky mickey instructions and believe it or not, we eventually arrived at the theater. The show itself was very glitzy…sort of Las Vegas, only covered up to the larynx, with lots of pop tunes, some of whom I recognized from tin-pan alley. There was no attempt at any English sub-titles, nor did there seem to be any need.

Signs in English were fairly common in Tokyo. In our hotel, there was something in the lobby called a toothbrash bending machine, and one of our girls brought back a shopping bag from a discount store that was quite provocative because one of the vowels in the "discount" was missing.

Eating in Tokyo restaurants was very simple because no language was required. Just finger pointing. All the dishes were displayed in full colour plastic replicas so that all you had to do was give the finger. That was my first introduction to Sushi, which I thought was live bait and I was looking for a place to spit it out. Nowadays back home, it's a weekly and sometimes twice or trice eating-out habit, with that special Wasabi mustard that clears up my sinuses in no time.

48 TAKE THE A TRAIN

That's A for acceleration. If you suffer from any claustrophobia, a trip on the Tokyo subway will bring it out in you, but the trip on the train to Osaka was un-crowded. Maybe Japanese were leery about its incredible speed. Mount Fuji flashed by in a couple of seconds. It seemed to me it took as long to travel from Tokyo to Osaka as it took you to read this paragraph. In comparison Via Rail is the Toonerville trolley.

49 SENRI HANKYU

That was the name of our Hotel. Sounds like Anglo-Japanese for Thank You, Henry. They had billeted the Charlottetown company close to the fair itself, with a good chance for the cast to visit before they were asked to perform. I remember the green tea ice cream they served at lunch, which startled me at first but I have since grown to love.

I was stuck in my hotel room doing "Turvey's" rewrites but I did manage to get out of my cell once in a while. There was only three years between our Montreal Expo and theirs, and since I am drifting into senility, I am hard pressed to differentiate between the two events. I do have hazy recollections of a film of the Musical Ride in a 360 degree all around theatre, a process which made them look like a firing squad ready to annihilate each other. The main thing I remember are the ever-present crowds, with little Japanese women elbowing their way through them with a determination that would make Gordie Howe very jealous.

50 OHIO DIANA!

No, we're not heading for a tour of the U.S.A. Ohio (I'm not sure of the way it's spelled) is Japanese for good morning, as long as its before noon, then the proper phrase becomes…hope I spell it right…Konicheewa.

Heading for the first matinee, I decided I would do what the Japanese were doing, rent a pair of earphones that would bring me Japanese sub-titles along with the English (sorry, Canadian) dialogue on stage. Amid the flurry of rapid foreign words, I recognized some improperly pronounced proper names like Marrirer, Girbert Brize and Missarynd.

I didn't see the Crown Princess. There was no particular fuss about her arrival or departure. But if she was like the rest of that audience she thoroughly enjoyed herself. That Expo exposure started a tourist wave of Japanese coming to Prince Edward Island. Mostly it was wives dragging their husbands along, and many of them got remarried in a special ceremony at George Campbell's Lucy Maud Museum, beside the Lake of Shining Waters on PEI's North Shore. The numbers fell off during the currency crisis of the late nineties, but they are coming back, especially young female tourists now that their economy has kicked in again.

51 BACKSTAGE SCUTTLEBUTT

For a different perspective on our Expo 70 adventure, I defer to Crew Chief Roddy Diamond. Roddy had to deal with the language barrier between his bunch and the Japanese crew. None of them spoke English but there were two translators provided by the Japanese management, one worked only with the carpenters and the other dealt solely with the electricians. There was also another kind of doubling. For every light cue the Charlottetown had designated, for instance a spot on the left, the Japanese electrician would create an equal light on the right, so that there were two complete sets, where only one was needed. Well, at least nobody was left in the dark.

One incident happened during the quick change upstairs in Anne's room, when she has to put on the green hair wig. One of the Japanese stagehands, a big fellow who must have been from the northern island of Hokkaido where they grow them tall, got caught in the bedroom as the little rooftop flat rose up and the scene began. Gracie, as Anne, was aware of his struggles to hide under the tiny bed she was on, but her main concern was that if

Barbara, as Marilla, saw the big lug she might freak out. Somehow this big fellow managed to make himself scarce during the whole bedroom scene and how he managed to get under that tiny bed, nobody will ever know.

There was a kind of camaraderie between the two crews which ended up in a kind of contest, a drinking contest to be exact. On closing night the Japanese crew took our Islanders out to a very exotic Osaka restaurant. Its interior looked like a jungle, covered in vines and there was even a pool in the middle of it. There was a long table provided for the crew's meal and a lot of eight ounce glasses, which were soon filled with Jack Daniels whisky, straight, no water.

The Japanese opened the challenge. Each one chug-a-lugged an eight ounce glass of whisky, downing the whole thing in one gulp. As soon as they finished, the Japanese filled them up again. In the space of four minutes the Japanese had consumed sixteen ounces. The Canadian crew were already feeling sick from the exchange and were looking around for a nearby tropical plant to pour their second glass of booze in it. It was no contest. Canadians had given the ultimate insult to their Japanese hosts. Instead of being offended, the Japanese enjoyed our boys discomfiture.

Then the food was brought in. Individual portions of jellyfish, the kind that most swimmers avoid on the beaches of Cavendish, followed by the piece de resistance, an entire octopus plopped on the table. One of our boys got so sick he dove into the restaurant pool and ruined a three hundred dollar suit. Another one surfaced at the hotel three days later. How unlike the home life of our own dear Anne.

52 RUBBERNECKING IN NIPPON

That's another name for Japan. Not rubbernecking, Nippon. And so is Yeddo, an even more ancient name. The cast took advantage of some time off to travel to places that were here when Yeddo was young, like Nara, which is about the holiest place in Japan, where there is a hundred and fifty foot reclining Buddha. Everybody wanted to visit Kyoto even before there was an Accord. And not the Honda one. Then there was Kobe, home of delicious Japanese beef, where the cows are fed regular dollops of beer and are massaged daily to keep their flesh tender.

I missed out on all of that, except for the beef which was doggy-bagged back to me at the hotel where I laboured over "Private Turvey's War," the new title of our musical. Norman and Elaine would check in on me after their touristic peregrinations. We dreamed up a song about the horrors of war to please our original author Earle Birney. It was called *"War is Hell Private Turvey, war is hell, war is healthy for the whole economy."* It would fit into a scene about the Belgian black market which dealt with both sides of the opposing forces.

For relief, I would watch bouts of Japanese television. In the daytime there were silly game shows, rather like the one I conducted on CTV for two years, called "Anything You Can Do," implying that women could do it better. It consisted of races where both sexes competed against each other by crawling backwards through the trap door in a pair on longjohns. The Japanese game show was very much like that, and the look of complete disdain on the faces of the husbands, as both sexes were made to make a foolish display of themselves in front of each other, was very revealing about the Westernization of Japanese culture. It was also great fun watching Lorne Greene on Bonanza spouting Japanese as if he was Toshiro Mifune.

On the good side of that first visit, the musical *"Anne of Green Gables"* has done it's share to foster good international relations. Our *"Anne of Green Gables"* has toured Japan four times, sometimes with the full company (1970–1991), sometimes with only four performers, Anne, Marilla, Matthew and Diana, on goodwill tours, like the one in 1989 for the Kelo Department Stores, and in 1993 for the Japan Travel Bureau.

53 BACK TO THAT OTHER ISLAND

Prince Edward that is. Not Honshu or Hokkaido or Okinawa.

The last day I spent in Tokyo, I saw a demonstration against the presence of the U.S. forces in Okinawa that dwarfed any organized protest I have ever seen. Thousands of young protesters, they looked like university students, marching through the center of the city. Post-war Japanese democracy brought by the Americans seemed to be working against the U.S.

Back home there were cast changes for our Festival. Barbara Hamilton was giving up the part of Marilla as a CBC television series was waiting to claim her. Mary Savidge took over the role playing it with a slight Scottish accent. I don't know what happened to Barbara's TV series but I was able to cast her as Valeda Drain Farquharson the following year on the TV series "Shhhhhh…it's the news." The provocative title was thought up by Norman Campbell who directed the pilot show for me, but was unable to continue because we did the show for CTV and he was contracted to CBC. CTV eventually decide the show was too CBC for their purposes and sold it to Global in their first year of operation.

Meanwhile back at the Festival ranch, Susan Anderson who had been Diana in both Charlottetown and London, announced that she was pregnant. This made her unacceptable for the part since nice Avonlea girls in elementary school don't get with child except for Prissy Andrews, but her teacher, Mr. Phillips, made the whole affair legitimate. Whether the child was born in or out of wedlock is something Lucy Maud and I never pronounced upon. In the production I just saw in 2007at the Grand Theater in London Ontario, the result was twins, a boy and a girl with matching blue and pink blankets. These were exhibited during the curtain call.

Susan Anderson's place was taken by Glenda Landry, another Charlottetown girl like Gracie Finley. As Anne and Diana the two had a remarkable chemistry between them. Like Roddy Diamond, Glenda had been an usher in the theater from its beginning. At the same time she was theatrically active with a local children's theater called Circus Tent directed by Ron Irving.

Glenda was auditioned for the part of Diana by a formidable panel consisting of Artistic Director Alan Lund, his assistant Lloyd Malenfant, arranger John Fenwick and Jack MacAndrew. Not only that, generous Gracie Finley did the audition with her.

Afterwards, shaking with nerves from the effort, Glenda went to Reddens drug store near the Center and had a stiff chocolate soda to wait for the verdict. As she was sipping the dregs of the soda, the straw made enough noise that Glenda did not notice Jack MacAndrew sliding onto the stool beside her, whispering in her ear "Hello Diana."

That was it. Eighteen year old Glenda Landry was to be Anne Shirley's kindred spirit Diana Barry for the next twenty two years. Time enough to get three teenagers of her own. While they were growing up, Glenda watched their antics and incorporated them into her own ever youthful performance. For example the way they stood on the sides of their feet was blended into their mother's stage character. She never stopped building on that character every year.

In 1992, the artistic director told her the time had come to play the older character, Mrs. Spencer, but she continued to understudy the part she had played for almost two decades. Heidi Ford, a formidable Diana Barry in her own right, told me that Glenda was the best Diana ever.

Fen Watkin told me about the time when Matthew was late to greet Anne from her first day at school. It was supposed to be after Anne says "excruciatingly, isn't that a scrumptious word. It took me weeks to learn how to say it right." Still no Matthew. So Anne ad-libbed to Diana "Do you know how to spell excruciatingly?" Diana's embarrassed pause and the audience laughter held until a late Matthew arrived on stage breathing hard.

Now Glenda is tickling the funny bones of Charlottetown audiences as the slightly ditzy Mrs. Spencer, who brings Anne to the Island instead of that boy the Cuthberts had requested. She has been a Festival fixture for thirty eight years, and long may she remain.

Glenda gives a lot of credit for the success of her audition to Alan's assistant, Lloyd Malenfant, who taught her the dances and the songs until one o'clock in the morning. She feels that Lloyd was really what held the production of *"Anne of Green Gables"* together for forty years.

Alan Lund was forced to give most of his attention to the new shows, but for *"Anne of Green Gables"* there was always Lloyd with his notebook searching for an empty seat off aisle two at the rear of the theater and making notes on each and every performance. Performers on stage sometimes noticed the little light on his pen go on and realized that they would probably get a note from this mother hen after the show. "Don't do that again."

Both Alan and Lloyd were determined to keep the gestures of the performers in *"Anne of Green Gables"* faithful to its turn of the century period. Nothing contemporary was allowed in their gestures. No hands on hips, no sticking out of tongues, no bratty behavior allowed.

Like the backstage crew, Glenda Landry has never gotten tired of doing the show, because as Glenda says "there is a new audience every night, and it's her job as a performer to show up every night with her A-game, prepared to give one hundred and ten percent. If you're writing your grocery list while on stage, then you have no business being there. Acting is listening." She added that " on matinee days, all you do between the afternoon and the evening performance is eat and sleep. The ritual is essential. You can't expect to get your energy from the audience, you have to create the energy for them."

Thirty eight years and counting. How lucky we have been to have a Glenda Landry in our midst. And too a Lloyd Malenfant. We lost Lloyd to a heart attack at his home in Victoria B.C. soon after he joined us in Charlottetown to celebrate the fortieth anniversary or our show. His care of our orphan will never be forgotten on stage or backstage.

54 NEW YORK, NEW YORK

The 1971 season featured a revival of last year's hit "Jane Eyre," plus a new musical "Mary Queen of Scots" and by now, the inevitable *Anne of Green Gables,* along with an invitation to bring it to New York. Jack MacAndrew had arranged for our show to appear in December at New York's City Center Theatre, home of many operatic productions. Neither Norman, Elaine or I were enthusiastic about such a drastic venture. Kevin Kelly of the Boston Globe had already panned our show, but Alan Lund shrugged it off. He said "today's reviews end up as wrapping paper for tomorrow's fish and chips."

Jack MacAndrew talked us into it. I had been too long on the Great White Way to think that a New York theatre audience would take to Anne. London, possibly, but New York, never. I have been at many Broadway opening nights and seen the brittle sophistication of first niters who were much more interested in being seen than seeing anything on that stage. Londoners were different, in their ratty fur stoles they wanted to see a show and enjoy it.

But the City Center wasn't exactly Broadway, so I breathed a little easier. It was the home of City Opera productions, as oppose to the Metropolitan. In addition, a lot of concert versions of former Broadway musicals were performed there, without sets, on a bare stage.

The preparations for our move to New York were not as complete as they should have been, especially regarding the dancers. The stage floor was wood, not linoleum, when Jeff Hyslop did his great slide during the shoe dance, he got a shard of wood in his thigh muscle. From that engagement on, the Festival touring company carried its own floor.

The crew and company stayed at the Goreham Hotel not far from the theater, with a warning to everyone never to venture out alone. Those were pre-Rudy Juliani days, the hero of 9/11, as he never tires of telling us, and there was general suspicion that he solved the problem of vagrancy by scooping up every bum, rubby, grifter and petty con man and bundled them all off to furthest Iowa.

Roddy Diamond got more than a stern warning about the perils of the big city when he met with his equivalent backstage at City Center. First thing the head stagehand said to Roddy was "You need protection." Out of a drawer came a gun, a switch blade and a pair of brass knuckles. Roddy quietly demurred. During the run there were some examples of violence. For some reason a stage doorman was beaten and left in a heap on the floor.

For Glenda Landry it was her first time away from PEI. She heard about a murder in her hotel top floor, not to mention the bordello in full operation on that same floor. Glenda was apprehensive about it all because her mother and grandmother were arriving for the opening.

The opening night television critics were brutal. They were on the phone to their producers forty five minutes after the curtain went up. "It's nuthin but a kid show. Not as good as our "Rebecca of Sunnybrook Farm." The print critics were far kinder, the Post and The Times were mild raves. This may have been because the dean of New York critics, Clive Barnes, had married a girl from Toronto's CBC, but it's quite possible he liked the show for its own sake.

The opening night party was given by Sally Brayley, a former Islander who had married a distinguished New Yorker. They gave us a party at their penthouse on Park Avenue just off Central Park. That night there was a gang shoot-out at the Sheraton, close to the Brayley's digs. I personally swear there was an unattended corpse lying on the curb when I got out of a taxi and hurried up an elevator that led directly to Sally's penthouse. In contrast to what was happening on the streets of New York, the living room floor was covered with plush white carpeting. Glenda Landry arrived with sixteen year old Calvin McRae in tow, because she had faithfully promised his mother that she would look after her son and heir. Calvin had his first taste of champagne…and threw up all over that white rug.

After the run of Anne at the City Center, both Gracie Finley and Glenda Landry were asked by the management to stay on in the U.S. with the idea of mounting a new American production of our musical. They both said "No thanks" and went back to the Island. Gilberts were more prone to saying yes to the siren call of Broadway. Three of ours ended up in "A Chorus Line"; Calvin McRae, Claude Tessier and Jeff Hyslop. Jeff went on to play the title role in the touring production of "Phantom of the Opera" and as mentioned, the London production of "Kiss of the Spider Woman."

55 COUNTERFEIT ANNES

I am told that there are at least five different musicals of *Anne of Green*

Gables" appearing at various times in different parts of the U.S. According to Marian Hebb, lawyer for the Lucy Maud estate, they are not allowed to use the title *"Anne of Green Gables"* because of our Dramatist Guild rights. For example there was a production in the spring of 2007 at the Lucille Lortel Theatre in Greenwich Village, the leading off-Broadway theater which housed "The Threepenny Opera" for several years. Their musical was called "The Bend in the Road" which is the title of the chapter in the novel where Matthew dies.

While I was visiting my grandchildren in Brooklyn and thought I should see the production for myself. But when I phoned the box office, three weeks after it opened, it was playing only on weekends. I missed out on seeing it, but it doesn't sound like much of a threat to our *"Anne."*

There was another production from Los Angeles called by the same title as ours and destined to play the prestigious Amandson Theatre. My daughter Kelley managed to get a copy of both script and score from the Internet. I'm hardly objective but I thought the whole thing was absolutely terrible.

There's also a mid-thirties non-musical play version of the novel by someone called Alice Chadwick that sounds very "by cracky" mid-West American. It's still around.

I hear there is a fly-by-night musical of *"Anne of Green Gables"* roaming around Japan, but Martin Naylor, our English representative in Tokyo, maintains that our official Japanese counterpart, Shiki Productions, is too busy or too lofty to care. Through the years Shiki has created four productions of *"Anne of Green Gables"* in Japanese and has confirmed that it will be on stage in Tokyo from February to June 2008 and then will proceed to tour the rest of Japan to celebrate the Centennial of the novel.

Meanwhile our *"Anne of Green Gables"* musical has been done by almost every high school in Canada, and is starting to appear in schools and summer camps in the United States. I suppose that's because it has no violence and is full of the family values the American right wing politicians keep talking about.

56 AND ON THE SAME BILL...

During its forty-four years with the Festival, our music has been teamed up with some pretty impressive rivals. In 1972 there appeared from Montreal a ghost story called "Ballade" with the most impressive score of any Festival musical. It played for two seasons until another formidable competitor came along. It was a re-working of Shakespeare's Hamlet, called "Kronborg 1564" by Cliff Jones. The date is the same as Shakespeare's birth, but Kronborg is neither the name of Hamlet's castle nor the name of his University. At any rate the show was a big success, and one popular number included a spoof on country music. It was repeated a second year and caught the attention of the well known Broadway choreographic team of Marge and Gower Champion. They took it to Broadway with an African-American actor in the leading role. After some major script and score changes to suit the American public, it also underwent a title change to "Rockabye Hamlet." It lasted only a week on the Great White Way.

On the other hand the Charlottetown "Hamlet" that year was Brent Carver, who successfully went on to Stratford-On-Tario where he distinguished himself as the original, non musical, Hamlet. Alas, he never was asked to take part in our *"Anne of Green Gables"* musical.

A couple of well known American actresses were asked to perform in our musical, both playing, of all things, the non-speaking role of Prissy Andrews, the teacher's girlfriend who was nuzzled by him at the back of the classroom. Beverley D'Angelo, who was also Brent Carver's "Ophelia" in Charlottetown. She later starred as the long suffering wife of Chevy Chase in that summer vacation film where everything goes wrong.

Another memorable Prissy Andrews was Andrea Martin, who went on to create Edith Prickly on Second City TV. She won a Tony Award for her portrayal of Aunt Eller in the Broadway revival of Oklahoma, and is now appearing as the German housekeeper in Mel Brooke's musical recreation of Young Frankenstein ("He vass mine boy friend"). Brian McKay was Mr. Phillips to Andrea's Prissy, and he told me that the laughter she caused in the picnic scene was so sustained that their passage across the stage in the three legged race took about six minutes.

57 TIME TO MOVE IN...

Excerpts from the life of Brian...McKay.

I joined the Charlottetown Festival Company, and the exalted cast of " *"Anne of Green Gables,"* " thirty six years ago. I refer to it as the "*exalted*" cast of *"Anne of Green Gables"* because in 1972 the cast list read like the Who's Who of Canadian Musical Theatre, and *that* cast had taken over their roles from the people who had *created* the Canadian musical theatre! So, for a kid of twenty-two with the proverbial stars in his eyes, it didn't, as they say, get any better.

I only performed in *"Anne of Green Gables"* for my first two seasons (of a total of eleven, as it turned out,) at the Festival. My second season saw me cast as Mr. Phillips (the school teacher) with Andrea Martin as Prissy Andrews, my partner in crime. Ms. Martin is, as everyone who has not spent the intervening years locked in a grain silo knows, one of the funniest and most celebrated performers in the business today: she is one of the most gracious and generous and also one of the most energetically mischievous individuals I have ever known. This led to numerous incidents occurring on and about the stage which I remember to this day and most of which I cannot relate in Mr. Harron's book: except to say that the Mr. Phillips/Prissy crossover at the end of the school picnic was more besotted with amorous passion (and more incriminating barn-straw sticking out of Prissy's costume and wig) than any production up until that time and quite possibly, to this very day.

But an incident that still causes me to cringe at the recollection (but was the cause of much mirth for the rest of the cast) occurred during a performance in which I was playing Earl, the Mailman. In my youthful exuberance (and perchance, ego), I put a good deal of thought into how I might make my interpretation stand out from the handful of other actors who had previously fleshed out the bones of this conqueror of hail, rain, sleet and snow. So, after careful examination of the possibilities, I opted out to play him as a chap of approximately one hundred and five or six years of (perpetually inebriated) age. To help with the aging, I decided to spray my hair white, and, as I never appeared without the hat, I eventually did so by putting tissue around the bottom of my mail-man's cap and spraying my hair while the hat was on. This worked wonderfully well until one particular night when I found myself in my dressing room having an engrossing conversation with one of the other actors.

There was nothing unusual about this except for the fact that the cue music for the General Store scene started playing over the backstage intercom, indicating the scene was about to start. That music, by the way, also indicated that I should be in the wings ready to go on, as I happened to be *in* that scene. Caught napping, I grabbed for my jacket and mailbag and broke speed records for land travel, making it to the wings just as the last of my four cast mates had given up hope of my arrival and were now praying for a power outage across the entire Island, thus saving me the outrageous embarrassment of missing an entrance. As I say, however, I made it at the very last instant and proceeded onstage, trying to pretend my stomach was not in danger of making its own surprise appearance.

As soon as I had taken two steps on the "deck," I realized from the growing reactions of my fellow and ever-stalwart cast mates that something was terribly amiss. It became frighteningly clear to me that, one by one, they had begun to avoid eye contact in places where it had always existed and I soon began to feel like Earl the ostracized mailman! Thoroughly professional to the last, they simply refused to look at me (at the time I didn't realize that they were, in fact, unable to look at me) until finally dear Cleone Duncan (playing Lucilla) took pity on me and through

*Brian McKay, Amanda Hancox, Dennis Thatcher, the Queen, Prince Phillip &
Alan Lund "A Royal Reception."*

Charlottetown Festival Archives

a glance—directly and piercingly—from my eyes to the top of my head. My hand instinctively followed her stare to its target and my confusion was replaced by a different kind of agony. In my haste to reach the stage, I had forgotten to put on the mailman's hat. There I stood, in front of a packed house, with a wrap of white hair circumnavigating the lower half of my head, atop of which was a dome of dark brown. The remainder of that scene felt longer than my career to that point. I considered myself lucky that, after the performance, I still had one.

...TIME TO MOVE ON

Gracie Finley had been Anne for six consecutive seasons. The usual tenure is three. She was marrying and moving to England with her groom so at the curtain call the orchestra played the Mendelsohn Wedding March. When she came back ten years later with three kids in tow, the orchestra greeted her with Brahms Lullaby.

Gracie's place was taken over by Malorie Anne Spiller who was with us for the next four seasons. Petite and almost regal in her bearing Malorie reminded a lot of people of the young Princess Elizabeth.

58 AUDITIONS

Every January, Norman, Elaine and I were asked by the resident artistic director to be present at Toronto's auditions for new talent. Norman showed his prowess as an actor by playing the role of Matthew to a series of actresses trying out for the role of Anne. Usually the auditions consisted of the opening scene at the railroad station leading into the song "Gee I'm Glad I'm No One Else But Me." Sometimes I would play the part of Mrs. Lynde, leading up to Anne's musical apology to her.

Leisa Way's recollection of her audition.

"Don, I'll never forget that audition. I was twenty years old. A kid from Sudbury, with no agent. I was small town green. Na!...I showed up where you were auditioning and I crashed the audition. I didn't even know what the term "crashed" meant. But I did it. I got there just after 9:00 a.m. and waited around until someone showed up to take names for the auditions, which began at 10:00 a.m. They took my name and made it very clear to me that crashers might not be seen. I waited all day. Of course being non-equity

Malorie Anne Spiller, Pierre Trudeau, Alexandre & Michel

member, even though I was the first crasher to arrive, equity crashers took priority over me.

I waited in the waiting room all day long, fascinated by the stream of actors who came through, professional actors, who were auditioning for the show. And finally, it was just past 6:00 p.m. because the auditions ran overtime that day. And you, Don came out of the room and walked by me again, (you had walked by me a few times during the day) and you noticed me, you looked at the stage manager and said "Has this little gal been here all day?" She disappeared into the room with you. About twenty minutes later, I was called into the room. The rest as they way is "Anne History."

She remembers the highlight of her time at the Festival was having had the chance to work with Liz Mawson. In her own words: "More than having a long and successful career, Liz embodied the grace, professionalism and good-natured attitude that we all attempt to achieve in our work and lives. She was a joy to act with, a wonderful role model and the most perfect

Marilla I have ever seen or imagined. I am grateful that I had the opportunity to share the stage with her in her final year of playing the role."

In 2002 we lost another outstanding Anne, Chilina Kennedy, who had brought fresh humour to the role for two beautiful years, because she was offered a role in the road company of "Mamma Mia," the money offered was too hard to turn down.

Her replacement was a young actress who had been part of the road company of "Mamma Mia," Jennifer Toulmin. She came in from Philadelphia where it was playing and was so exhausted by the journey to Toronto that she fell asleep on the bench outside the rehearsal room. We had to wake her up to do the audition. It turned out that Jennifer was a worthy successor to the talented Chilina, with the same comic inventiveness. She became our Charlottetown Anne for the next four years, and reprised her role in successful appearances in Drayton, Penetang and London's Grand Theatre. Miss Toulmin still manages to look as if she's about twelve years old.

Jennifer Toulmin & dog
"Anne and another kindred spirit"

But the audition journey from Philadelphia to Toronto pales beside the miles undertaken by our current Anne, Amy Wallis. She came on her own all the way from Victoria, B.C. on the off chance that we might approve of her as our young leading lady. Amy did the required two numbers plus the dialogue. Before we could let her know she had the part, she was off to the airport and back to Victoria. Our latest Anne found out the good news as soon as she got in the door back home.

59 AN IMAGINARY HORSE WITH A BUGGY BEHIND

Anne's first song takes place in a carriage driven by Matthew, usually horseless. David Hughes has played Matthew in Charlottetown, Stirling Festival

Theatre, Stage West and on tour in Japan. The buggy ride has always loomed large in his attempt to guide it across the stage. This is how he related the problems to me: "The first time for me was on the Charlottetown stage. My eye was immediately caught by the sight of a stagehand crouched down in the wings, an intent look on his face, as he slowly cranked the cable that pulled the buggy across the stage. It was tricky. The speed had to be exactly timed so that Anne's song "Gee I'm Glad…"would be ending just as we disappeared into the wings. It also had to be guided so as not to run into the front drop, nor get too close to the edge of the stage. What soon took my mind off the stagehand was the magic of Anne's singing. That first time, and in fact every time since, I've been entranced at how such a beautiful sound can pour out of someone's mouth. I'm not a singer myself, so needless to say I've always found it mesmerizing."

At Stage West, a dinner theater in Mississauga, the stage was built into a corner, which meant there was very little room onstage, our buggy just clearing the front drop. During one performance, the front corner of the buggy caught on the porch of the house. The stage hand was struggling with his crank trying to get it to clear, but it was of no use. The song was coming to an end, and we still had ten feet to go to get to into the wings. I said something like "It's alright, we'll walk the rest of the way" and we did. With luck, the audience assumed that was the way the scene was suppose to end.

"In Stirling, the designer had cleverly adapted an electric wheelchair to build a buggy around, which meant no crank and cable were necessary. However it made life a little more difficult for me. This meant it was me, not a stagehand who had to get the timing right during our journey across the stage. The other problem was that the only light on stage was from a follow-spot. Everything else was in complete blackness. There wasn't even a light visible from the wings where we were headed. It was a bit like driving down a country road at night without headlights and a blinding white light shining in through the side window. I was hoping we were not too far from the wings when I happened to look down and saw the startled faces of a couple of people in the front row. We were just inches away from the edge of the stage. I made a sharp turn away in what I hoped was the right direction and at that moment the assistant stage manager pulled aside the curtain masking the wings and we made it off safely. Stage make-believe is a wonderful thing, but where is Pearl, Matthew's invisible horse when you need her?"

60 ON THE ROAD AGAIN

Most reports I get of touring versions of *"Anne of Green Gables"* contain two basic elements, a box office statement and a list of backstage disasters encountered by our crew.

In one instance, the storage space was so small inside the theater that the Act II props and extra set had to be placed outside in the alleyway. Luckily it didn't rain.

During a 1986 tour in Vancouver B.C., one of the local stagehands got hit when he ran into the edge of the porch during a three man set-up for Anne and Diana's drunk scene. He knocked himself out and the scene began with no one noticing that there was a body lying on stage. Nobody in the general public complained about this new twist in the plot.

On a visit to Windsor, Ontario, the truck provided to transport the sets was so small that they had to put the picket fence on top of the truck. The weather was not the best and by the time the truck got to the theater, the fence was black and had to be scrubbed down.

61 YOUTH MUST HAVE ITS TURN

One of the things I'm getting used to is seeing children in the adult roles of our musical. First time I encountered it was at Camp Tawingo near Hunstsville, run by my college buddy Jack Pearse. I have sent all three of my daughters there, but none of them participated in a production in which Matthew was played by a fourteen year old boy, Marilla by a mature fifteen year old and Anne outranked them all at sixteen.

Oshawa Little Theatre has a children's theater wing and their production a couple of years ago upped the age quotient to about twenty while Anne was a snub nosed freckle faced darling of thirteen. This concept does nothing to destroy the basic story even if Matthew's voice sometimes gives squeaking evidence of going through the changes.

As mentioned earlier, Toby Tarnow was Anne in the very first musical of Anne, the ninety minute version of the 1956 TV version,. Toby now lives in Hollis, New Hampshire with her husband Richard, in a wonderful two hundred year-old house, the kind that has a fireplace in every room. Toby has matured gracefully into a slim beauty. And for the past few years, she has made annual visits to PEI and we've had several reunions in the Campbell's summer home in Covehead.

Don, Toby & Elaine "A Golden Occasion"

For the past couple of years, Toby has been involved with a children's theatre in a nearby New Hampshire town. In 2006 she produced and directed a highly professional children's production of our "*Anne*". The girl in the title role had more than a few of the elements that had made Toby an Anne Shirley that will never be forgotten.

Toby has added another element to her children's theater where she encourages the children to create their own plays. In the summer of 2007 Toby conducted a course in play-making with a class of sub-teen kids at the Charlottetown Festival facilities with great success. The average age was twelve, most were ten years old, there were only two boys in the group. She had exactly one week to get her little group ready to appear in public.

Their assignment was to improvise two different plays, choreograph and stage their play, and make their costumes. And different they were indeed. The first play was a gothic fairy tale involving dark goings on, Hamlet like intrigue in the kingdom of Ireland. The second was a satiric recreation of the television series Canadian Idol. The two plays were performed out of doors, in the space usually occupied everyday at day at noon by the Charlottetown Young Company, in front of a small but appreciative audience.

Annie Allan, the artistic-director has pledge that this successful experiment will be repeated next summer.

62 THE BEND IN THE ROAD

Toby's brief hour upon that outdoor stage is something I will always remember because I had just come from Elaine Campbell's hospital room. Claudette and I hadn't seen much of Elaine during the summer of 2006 because she was feeling poorly. Her children had gathered from all points of the compass and were very protective. As well they should.

Our reunion in the hospital on that Friday August 10th was joyful. We talked about the beginnings of *"Anne of Green Gables"* back in '56 and how much we both missed her husband Norman. We laughed and made plans to go to Stratford and Shaw Festivals the following month. That fateful night she passed away.

We didn't get the awful news till the next morning while driving through New Brunswick, having just left the Island. Her son Rob said "I felt that mom was ready to go.." Claudette, said it best: "Norman had written some heavenly music and he needed the best lyricist he knew."

Because we were on our way back to Toronto, we missed the gathering of friends at the house in Covehead, the beautiful home that looks so much like Green Gables. However we attended the celebration of her life at the Glenn Gould Studio, in the CBC headquarters in Toronto. The same type of celebration had been done for Norman in 2004, in the ballroom of the now defunct Toronto's Inn on the Park, where Fen Watkin provided the piano rendition of Norman Campbell's music.

During the opening remarks at his father's celebration of life by the eldest son, Robin, (the one carried in his mummy's tummy while she wrote the lyrics "Gee I'm Glad I'm No One Else But Me") the lights in the room started flickering, Rob looked upward and interrupted his speech with the remark "Dad is still running this show, and he doesn't like the lighting."

Justine sang "I'll Follow" the love ballad from our musical "Private Turvey's War," the warm and tender lyrics were written by Elaine. In 2006, Justine sang it again, playing the role of Peggy, in a one night presentation of the musical as part of Jim Betts's Script Lab week of Canadian musicals at the Todmorden Mills Theatre. This fulfilled Norman's last request to me as he handed me the "Turvey" script: "Get it on." I'm still trying dear Norman. 2009 is the seventieth anniversary of World War II, so I'll try again.

Melissa, the first daughter, made a witty speech about her own attempts to rival her parent's accomplishments.

Geoff Campbell had flown from San Francisco where he works for George Lucas in computer graphics. (The skeleton crew in Pirates of the Caribbean is his fine work). He was brief and to the point, suppressing his grief.

The youngest, Nicholas, bound up to the stage, proceeded to give a hilarious account of his early life in the Campbell household wearing the much too big jacket of Norman's.

Jennifer Toulmin, the then current Charlottetown Anne, sang the title song *"Anne of Green Gables."* After which Sid Adilman, Veronica Tennant and myself spoke a few words. Fen played "Wond'rin" and Jennifer sang "Gee I'm Glad I'm No One Else But Me."

Every one there was asked to join in singing *"Anne of Green Gables."* A warm and emotional rendition by all. Norman would have loved it.

The celebration of life for Elaine on October 23rd 2007 was well attended by family and friends. Again the children were in charge of things. On a big screen for the whole world to see were the many faces of Elaine, her brilliant smile, her sense of fashion, her joie de vivre, from her earliest days. A superb job of collecting photographs of their mum from her days in the RCAF uniform, some glamorous shots at openings of the National Ballet, Jane Austen conventions, quick snapshots in Europe, Japan and her many trips abroad and finally that summer home in Covehead where Norman used to address the neighbouring herd of cows: "My fellow citizens, unaccustomed as I am to public speaking…."

The speeches by the Campbell progeny were warm and funny as usual.

Nick again did his kooky off-the-wall speech which was a warm funny way of telling the world he adored his mum.

The final speech was given by Jamie, Elaine's teen-age grandson. The words were so wonderful that I asked Melissa, his mother, and Jamie himself for permission to reproduce them in the pages of this book. By the way, this teenager refers to himself in his e-mail as Captain James Campbell-Prager.

Here it is: verbatim.

Can you hear me out there? Well you're not missing anything.

I was originally going to sing, but I hummed it to myself and realized that no one wants to hear that. Anyway, it's a rather obscure tune of Tom Lehrer's, so I think I'll pass on that. At one in the morning last night, I had what used to be called an epiphany, but is nowadays referred to as insomnia, and this whole idea came to me in the basement, on the couch, where it's cold, so please keep in mind it was conceived at one a.m. So if it doesn't make sense, please bear with me and smile politely when you see me later.

You hear a lot these days about time management. You have to plan for both your short term and your long term, and make sure you know exactly where you're going, but I don't really think my grandmother ever had to do that because she knew how to live in the now. There's a phrase "we are here and this is now," and my grandmother understood that better than anyone I've ever met. She could know exactly where she was in time, she knew exactly what paths to take, and at eighty-three she stood in Leptis Magna, in Libya, one of the most closed countries of the twentieth century. She fulfilled one of her oldest dreams, and she must have felt like a Roman General receiving his triumph in Rome, standing amongst the faded ruins of a glorious civilization. She must have just been grinning because that's the kind of person she was.

Along with time, the other thing she understood so well was that core tenet of her faith, which is "Deus est Amor" "God is Love." And if God is Love, then love is God and if God is everywhere, then love must be everywhere and she could pick up on that. She could go into a room of total strangers and come out knowing their life stories, who they were, their trials and tribulations and what made them laugh. And she could laugh along with them with that outrageous laugh of hers that you could hear from a house away, that would echo down the corridors, that high pitched shriek of joy she had. It would wake you late at night when you least expected it.

She could use those two forces together, her knowledge of time and her ability of love and accomplish what she did but….we can only dream of doing what she did. We can only dream that at eighty-three we will stand among the ruins of a city we've longed to be visiting, we can only dream of raising five functional kids in an era known for its dysfunction. We dream that we too can accidentally snub Lord Snowdon at the Royal Gala. Well, maybe it's just my dream, but it makes a good anecdote.

If there is one thing I'm going to miss, it's the way she used those two things. The way she could enter a room in that indomitable way of hers, that humble way, with everyone just loving her. It's not something you see anymore. It's fast disappearing, that sense of faith, that sense of joy in the world and the people you meet. We shall not see her like again. We're not going to have another Elaine in our lifetime....I don't think my generation will produce another Elaine Campbell to reach for those goals from such humble beginnings, to love people the way she did and know where she was in time and what paths to take....if we can't even try to keep that faith, if we let it go, then we've committed a terrible crime: because she stood for such wonderful things, it's what she did so well...to take those steps...and I think we're all going to miss that, when we realize what's gone from our lives. The rest is silence, you know?

(Note: Jamie admits that his opening line is a quote from Groucho Marx)

Charlotte Moore then sang the title song from our last musical "The Wonder of It All" and Jennifer Toulmin repeated "Gee I'm Glad I'm No One Else But Me" Both Jennifer and Charlotte had come from *"Anne of Green Gables"* rehearsals in London, Ontario

For the whole production of "Wonder of it All" Elaine is the sole lyricist, and it's another project for me, to make sure that it will be seen on stage in the near future.

63 NOT SO MEMORABLE

Norman and Elaine were indefatigable about amateur productions of *"Anne of Green Gables."* If it was at all possible they attended every one, and always brought that sunny, optimistic disposition they both shared. Norman said there was always something fresh to learn from the interpretations of amateur actors.

Almost always anyway.

I will refrain from identifying the culprits but my composer and his lyricist wife once got trapped in what they said was the worst production they had ever seen. It wasn't the fault of the school kids who performed it. They had been misdirected by some would-be maestro Norman described as a three-chord wonder. Elaine and Norman said they slunk down in their seats for most of the so called performance. Elaine summed it up with "Golly, we didn't think a thing like this would ever happen."

I can go one better. Without identifying the source, I was sent a plane ticket to a remote (to me) part of Northern Ontario. Naturally I accepted with gratitude the invitation to see their production. When I got to the high school where it would be presented, I was introduced to two, not one, but two directors. This is not an unusual arrangement. Very often, even at Charlottetown, there was a director plus a choreographer.

However, in this case one director was a male English teacher and a female Music teacher was the other director. Nowhere was there a mention of a choreographer. What I sensed was an air of decided frostiness between the two of them. They left me to go backstage and the production began.

At first, things seem to move along as usual. The ladies of Avonlea were crisp in the enunciation of the lyrics of the opening number "We Are Great Workers For the Cause" and "Where Is Matthew Going." This was done in front of a velvet curtain. The curtain parted to reveal the inevitable orphan sitting on her suitcase as Matthew enters checking his watch. There was nothing wrong with the scene that followed. It was an adequate performance. The trouble started when Matthew invited Anne for a ride in the buggy.

Immediately four large high school boys appeared on the floor of the auditorium dragging an ancient…ahh…no, not a buggy…no…if I recall properly…it was more like…an authentic real-life down-to-earth wagon used for getting in the hay. These four young men, dressed as horses, lifted this heavy contraption onto the stage. From their groans it sounded like Operation Hernia. Then they proceeded to attach themselves to the traces in front of this lumbering wagon.

All the while Matthew and Anne stood by with nary a line of dialogue between them. This silence may have lasted all of two minutes but to me it seemed to stretch into oblivion.

Shall I go on…? I think not.

The war between the English and Music departments, each unassailable in their own fiefdoms, made the stage life of *Anne of Green Gables* extend to four and a quarter hours. Because they had bought my plane ticket, I was asked to join the cast's curtain call on stage and make a few remarks. I got up there with a red face and lied like a politician. "Well….ahh….this evening has been…ahh… really something." Then I went straight to anecdotes about the origins of our musical.

This is not the only horror evening I have spent. There was a production in Toronto and they had invited me to a rehearsal a week before they opened. It seemed like a good production and I gave them a few notes and suggestions. A week later I attended the opening of their production and found that none of my suggestions had been followed. That's par for the course but the thing that unnerved me was the girl who was playing Anne. I had been vaguely complimentary at rehearsal but it must have gone to her head. I don't know if she was deliberately playing to me in the front row but she never took her eyes off the audience the whole time, she did not relate to anyone in the cast. I bolted out of my seat as soon as the curtain came down. Elaine and Claudette were waiting for in me in the lobby, thinking that perhaps I was talking with people in the cast or maybe took some extra time in the washroom, but I was nowhere to be found. Unbeknown to them I had run away and was hiding down the street where the car was parked.

64 MULTIPLE CASTING

Nancy White, that writer of satiric songs like "Stickers on Fruit" was the first reviewer of our stage musical in Charlottetown back in 1965. She is also the composer and lyricist of "Anne and Gilbert" the sequel to our musical. Nancy has a daughter who attended Wexford Collegiate. Wexford is one of those showbiz schools that emphasize the performing arts in addition to their academic courses. There was an equivalent series about such a school on American TV called "Fame" with the theme song "I Wanna Live Foh Evah." I accepted the invitation to see her daughter with a slight trepidation because it followed soon after my two unfortunate experiences. I assumed her daughter was playing the role of Anne but such was the not the case, she was in one of the minor roles but Nancy wanted me to see the entire production which she described as unusual.

The first surprise was the opening number with the ladies from the church. There are four of them according to the script, but this production had twelve of them on stage, with varying ethnic members, when the line came about helping the lot of the Hottentot it was sung sweetly by a young woman they refer to now as an African-Ontarian.

Things proceeded normally until the meeting of the postman with the farmer, namely Earl and Cecil (pronounced Seesill). Immediately a whole bunch of vigorous young high school boys bounded on stage each one calling out either 'Mornin Earl" or "Mornin Cecil." I didn't count how many there were or who finally got to say the line "mainland's bin cut off agin," I have a feeling it was chanted in unison. The whole exchange was an absolute delight.

This time it was a privilege to be asked to speak on stage during the curtain call and I expressed the feeling that I wanted to take all of them with me to Charlottetown for the summer. Nancy White's pi-anna player, Bob Johnson, was the musical director and he sent me an audio tape of the whole experience, and I treasure it.

Another mass cast experience was when the Randolph Academy of Dramatic Art (housed in the former Bathurst Street United Church, the building in which I was baptized) put on our *Anne of Green Gables* musical. The multiple casting was designed to give every pupil of the graduating class a chance to show their stuff. Again it worked out well. And the Academy didn't stop there. They had a show going on before *Anne of Green Gables* even started. Various young ladies in period dress were in the lobby and the auditorium hawking their own preparation of raspberry cordial. It was such a pleasure for Elaine Campbell and I to go backstage and congratulate the cast. The young actors were pleased and surprised to talk with the living and breathing creators of the show.

The most unusual example of multiple casting that I have encountered so far was at a high school production in Calgary. I remember the woman who wanted to adopt Anne, Mrs. Blewett, had about twenty kids. But the real mass casting occurred during the picnic scene at the end of the first act, where everyone sings the "Ice Cream" song. All of a sudden the stage was filled to overflowing with high school kids. I learned later that there were two hundred and fifty young persons on stage for that first act finale. The reason? The parents were in the audience and all the kids wanted to be seen as part of the act. "Anne of Team Gables"???

65 CAREER HIGH

I was Master of Ceremonies sharing duties along with Mistress of Ceremonies, prima ballerina Veronica Tennant, for the twenty fifth anniversary of Canadian Actor's Equity. I have been a member of American Equity since 1951. During the course of the evening, Veronica asked me what I considered my greatest achievement. I paused for a moment, looking out at the audience who were all Actor's Equity members, and I said: "My greatest achievement has been my involvement with a musical that has given jobs to ten thousand professional actors."

Now that I recall my remarks, I realize that Anne gave much more than a job to many of those actors. It is also friendships that have stayed with them all these years. Friendship and a sense of family when those Anne performers were literally cast together for a whole summer. Leisa Way expresses what I am trying to say: "Lorraine Foreman is one of those special friends. We shared a house each year for many years in Charlottetown, and even though she was thirty-plus years older than me, our friendship was like that of two girlhood friends. It still is. We get together and time slips away. We can share anything and talk about anything."

Chilina Kennedy recalls a special episode this way. "One afternoon, as Heidi Ford and I were walking home from a matinee, we paused in front of Cows Ice Cream on Queen Street. A young Japanese tourist, who was by herself, had just purchased a delicious, fresh ice cream cone to enjoy in the heat of the late summer day. She didn't speak very much English and was attempting to figure out how to call a taxi. We asked her if there was anything we could do to help her and she said yes, could we please help her use the pay phone to call a taxi. Heidi took the piece of paper with the number on it and proceeded to make the call which left the tourist and I together on the sidewalk. We looked at each other for a moment and I was about to begin making polite conversation when suddenly her eyes widened with either fear of blind panic, I didn't know which and she screamed "You Annnnnneeeeee! AAAAAAHHHHH." She then leaped past me, threw her brand new ice cream cone, which she hadn't had a bite of, in the garbage and threw her purse on the ground in order to find her camera. The next fifteen minutes consisted of getting Heidi off the phone, another series of scream and incomprehensible sounds when our tourist found out Heidi was Josie Pye and many pictures, lots of jumping up and down and thank-yous for helping her followed."

Chilina continued: "It's amazing that young women come all the way from Japan to see the show, and it humbles me to be reminded how much the story of *"Anne of Green*

Chilina Kennedy and "Akage No An" Fans

Charlottetown Festival Archives

Gables" moves people, and even sometimes to do crazy things in the middle of the street. I'm also glad I that I had the chance to play this part and that I met the love of my life on this island. He is the grandson of the "real" *Anne of Green Gables,"* the adopted cousin of Lucy Maud herself. My husband Fenner's grandmother was Ellen, a home girl from England, who came over to Nova Scotia and was adopted by Pierce and Rachel Macneill of Cavendish, who lived across the road from what is now Green Gables. They originally wanted a boy but got Ellen. The cherry tree outside her bedroom window exists today. My husband showed it to me."

66 BLANKET DISAPROVAL

During the reign of Curtis Barlow, an Ottawa diplomat with such an elegant manner, that I think I use the noun reign appropriately, our artistic director ran into trouble with Joe Sark, chief of the Micmac Band on PEI's "Lennox Island." We were approaching the fortieth anniversary of our musical and never had trouble of any kind with Canada's first families. When Joe Sark saw the school pageant near the end of the show, or maybe somebody who had seen it and told him about it, the fertilizer hit the fan. The young lad who played the Indian in the pageant, making his rude forest home from some silver birch, was draped in a blanket. Standard costuming we thought. Not to Joe Sark. The blanket was something the white man had given to the aboriginals, and it carried the white man's disease, small pox, which cost many aboriginal lives. I didn't have anything to do with what the kid wore in the pageant, but as a Canadian historian, Charlie Farquharson's Histry of Canada, 1972, I should have known better. Sorry Chief Sark. Our actor now appears topless and blanketless.

67 STRINGS ATTACHED

One of the Islanders who got to run the Festival for a short time, was an amiable Oldsmobile salesman from Summerside, called Wayne Carew. Obviously a man careful with his pennies, for one of his first acts was to suggest changing the nineteen person orchestra into a six piece band with a couple of synthesizers. Norman Campbell rose up in wrath, something he did not Normanly do.

There is a moment just before Matthew dies which needs a violin and cannot be created by a mere machine. The original Matthew, Peter Mews, created a special moment with the orchestra by taking his last deep breath at the top of a violin arpeggio which seemed to wait for that intake of breath. When the lights go down on the slumped figure in the rocking chair, it's those other violins who do the work. I hear the results in the blackout that follows, by the unsnapping of female purses in a frantic search for the Kleenex.

After Norman left us, Elaine carried on the fight to keep the orchestra intact. She initiated a special fund which helps pay for the extra strings which are so necessary. Myself and some other people still contribute to that fund.

May our *"Anne of Green Gables"* have strings attached forever.

68 UPPERS AND DOWNNERS

The *"Anne of Green Gables"* team, Norman, Elaine and I, have written another musical about the life of Canadian painter Emily Carr. To me she was a West Coast *"Anne of Green Gables."* Orphaned early in her teens, Emily spend many years in frustration trying to fulfill her ambition of being accepted as a professional artist.

Later in her life, when she was more than fifty years old, Marius Barbeau, a cultural anthropologist, found one of Emily's paintings in a Haida grave and made his way to Victoria to seek her out. The result was an awakening of her long dead career as a painter and an acceptance by the Group of Seven, Canada's premier group of landscape artists.

I wrote the script based on Emily's own writings. Norman as usual composed the music but this time his wife Elaine wrote all the lyrics. "The Wonder Of It All," a direct quote from Emily when she first saw the B.C. forest, was first presented on the CBC TV network in 1972, and several years later, at the request of some theater people in Victoria, we did a stage version of our TV show. It was performed for three summers in Victoria at the museum that housed Emily Carr's paintings.

When I suggested to Wayne Carew that he read the script, he agreed. His reaction surprised me. "It's such a downer" he said. "No Wayne" I said "it's an upper. It ends in triumph for a woman who overcomes all the negatives and is destined for a bright future as one of Canada's great painters and writers." Emily Carr was awarded the Governor General's award for her first book, "Klee Wyck." I went further, "Wayne, it's *"Anne of Green Gables"* that is the downer, the whole thing ends with a funeral."

69 IS ANYTHING MORE DELECTABLE THAN... COOL-WHIP?

Cool-Whip that's what the ice cream in the Act One picnic finale is made of. Jenny Toulmin said: "The oil in the product holds its shape longer than real ice cream would, it also clumps better on my face."

Andrea Pachenko, "Anne of Cool Gables"

Trevor Black

Paul Smitz, props master at the Charlottetown Festival for many years, is in charge of its preparation and it can be complicated. You get the cool-whip out of the freezer and transfer it to the fridge. If you forget that transition, the cool whip is hard as a rock and could cause damage to the pretty young face of our leading lady. Either run it under a hot water tap or put it in the microwave oven for thirty seconds.

Once there was a young backstage apprentice, (he shall remain nameless), who insisted on taking a lick of the cool-whip cone before it left Paul Smitz's hands to the waiting grip of Gilbert Blythe. This stopped happening when Paul constructed a fake cone and filled it with shaving cream. Holding the real article behind his back Paul presented the fake one to the eager fingers of the backstage apprentice. As you can imagine there was a choking sound of someone gagging. That was the end of that episode.

70 CHANGE OF COMMAND

There came a time after many years of steering the good ship Charlottetown when Alan Lund left to continue his work in other ports of call. Whether it was his own decision or not, I have been unable to find out. His first stop was in Drayton, Ontario, where he initiated a show called "Vaudeville." It was so successful, it has been repeated more than once. To this day Drayton theater still celebrates an "Alan Lund Week" every year. Charlottetown should do it as well. Alan's devotion to our musical was complete: it was the very first musical he had ever directed after a series of revues like "Spring Thaw," and guided his choice of career for the rest of his days.

Back in 1986 Alan's place as Artistic Director was taken by Walter Learning, who had made an admirable reputation for himself at Fredericton's Theatre New Brunswick. Walter felt that Alan had made a cartoon out of our musical and was determined to redress the balance.

He arrived fresh from a Vancouver Playhouse production of "Chorus Line," choreographed by Jeff Hyslop, our former Gilbert to Gracie Finley's Anne. Walter brought Jeff with him as the new choreographer and Max Reimer was promoted from Cecil the farmer to Business Manager.

First thing the Learning-Hyslop team did was to change the opening of the show with the church ladies and their merry little ditty about the board of foreign missions. Walter and Jeff began the evening with a mime sequence on a bare stage in which the concept of "orphan" would be realized by a male actor called Todd Stuart who playing a cripple, wandered on stage, obviously lost and in need of help.

This symbol-minded approach seemed to me to be more Ibsen than Lucy Maud.

When asked about his reactions to it, Norman Campbell quoted a line from Anne: "You have hurt my feelings excruciatingly."

It didn't take Walter Learning more than a season to readjust his concept closer to Alan Lund's and our original version. Max Reimer, who was not only an experienced business manager, but also an adagio dancer specializing in lifts, became choreographer for the next five seasons. Max says that during the next season Walter kept saying to the dancers "Keep practicing that," and "I'll be back in a minute" and running back to the tape machine in his office that had Alan Lund's choreography. (Blanche Lund might not agree with its authenticity).

It was a Learning process for Walter and he took it well and went on to take more than one tour of Festival actors to Japan.

First thing artistic director Annie Allan did when she took over the reins of the Festival in 2004 was to contact Alan's widow, Blanche Lund, the other formidable half of a marvelous ballroom dance team that brightened up the

DON HARRON

wartime Navy Show and the first season of Canadian TV. Annie Allan is a top choreographer in her own right, worked with Harold Prince in several Broadway shows, but she wanted to reinstate all of Alan's original choreography with Blanche's help and was ably assisted by a former Gilbert, Jimmy White.

71 ANNE IN THE DARK

Leisa Way remembers the night of the big storm in 1990. "We had been warned of a horrific rain storm hitting town, and my Mom and Dad were visiting. Our director, Walter Learning was kind enough to come over just before the show with candles for Mom and Dad who were staying at my home that night. Walter was worried that they would be stuck in the dark, should the power go out. Walt and my Dad were great fishing buddies, even though my Dad was about 20 years older than Walt."

"Well, we made it almost all the way through the show that night and just before Liz Mawson's character Marilla sings "I Can't Find The Words" to Matthew's empty chair, the power went out in the entire theatre." Leisa continues: "I dare anyone who has seen *Anne of Green Gables* to tell me that Liz Mawson singing that song wasn't the most magical part of the show for them on a regular show night. From the first day I heard Liz sing it, talking to that sad empty chair, I struggled every night as an actress to hold myself together and not completely lose it. I would stand in the wings and most nights I couldn't watch her without my eyes welling up, let alone listen to her beautiful, heartfelt rendition of it, the words themselves were so honest and powerful."

But that night as the power went out, the emergency lights came up at the very back of the theater, however the entire stage was in complete darkness. The crew went running for flashlights and the dialogue continued in the blackness. When the orchestra started playing "I Can't Find the Words" the crew had found enough flashlights that enable them to stand in the wings and shine these small beams of light onto Liz's face as she sang that song."

"Well, on that particular night the audience was blessed with a version that would never be replicated. The power of the sight of just those small beams of light shining on her face was unbelievable and indescribable. There was a hush over the entire audience when she had finished, their own emotions were laid bare, they were speechless."

96

We continued into the last scene, with just those flashlights shining on our faces. It was an unforgettable evening of theatre for that audience and for us. The audience rose together to their feet at the end, cheering. It was an amazing feeling to look out into the darkness and feel such a powerful connection to an audience."

"When the curtain came down, our stage manager yelled: "Stay where you are" They only had so many flashlights and since our dressing rooms and hallways were dark, we were escorted in groups, and one by one to our dressing rooms. The theatre was a spooky place to be in the dark, yet none of us was scared. We all felt like we had shared something magical that night."

72 PELVIS PRESSING MATTERS

The biggest rival our *"Anne of Green Gables"* musical ever had at the Charlottetown Festival was Walter Learning's production of "Are You Lonesome Tonight" book and lyrics by Alan Bleesdale, an English writer who gave us his version of the story of the rise and fall of Elvis Presley. Most of it was fall, rather than rise.

There were two Elvises: the young hip-gyrating one who caused a sensation on the Ed Sullivan Show, and the overweight drug-taking Presley whose career suffered after the rise of the Beatles.

Young Elvis was played very hip-manipulating and with great dexterity by young fellow named Ben Bass. He became the magnet for groupies lining up at the stage door. The older Elvis was an actor I had seen at Stratford as a very regal and convincing Henry VIII, Leon Pownall.

Here is Leisa Way's impression of this distinguished actor: "Leon apparently could be a bugger to work with, as he showed in the show "Are You Lonesome Tonight" (very temperamental and diva-ish…for a man!) but I was very lucky. When I arrived in Charlottetown in 1987, I was sooooooo green…young and naïve…just starting out in the business. Leon was a seasoned Shakespearean actor, who could have walked ALL over me—-and from the rumours I heard—usually WOULD have. But! I have never worked with a more generous actor on stage. As Matthew, he was so generous with me, so much fun to work with and he taught me a lot—especially since I also played "Pricilla" to his Elvis in the other show, so sometimes we'd do a matinee of Anne and then go into the evening show where he played a drug addicted Elvis and we had a screaming divorce scene together!"

Elvis and Matthew. In Charlottetown double casting is an art. Does the mind not boggle? Never mind. The slovenly Mrs. Blewett is usually played by the same actress who is the elegant Mrs. Barry or the winsome Miss Stacy. Last season, a farm boy from Manitoba, Gerrad Everard played an hysterically funny Mick Jagger in "The British Invasion," and on alternate nights he was the demure, calm minister supervising the picnic races in our *Anne of Green Gables."* Janet McEwen's staid Marilla became a rockin' sex bomb on those same alternate nights.

The script of Elvis contained a problem, it was the f…word, which doesn't appear in *Anne of Green Gables."* A member of the Festival's Board panicked when she learned that the infamous word was to be uttered on the stage of the Charlottetown Festival. Jack MacAndrew knew what to do. He had the orchestra play very loud when the actor was uttering the forbidden noun, verb or adjective.

The Elvis "Are You Lonesome Tonight" musical ran for two seasons. The first year it registered well over ninety percent in attendance, leaving *Anne of Green Gables"* limping along in the mid-eighties. The second year there was a new older Elvis, Frank McKay. In the previous season he had done silent duty as one of Elvis the Elder's bodyguards. Frank's considerable vocal skills caused the Festival production to include Elvis's Las Vegas presentation of The Battle Hymn of the Republic. It was the high point of the show. Despite this outstanding vocal performance the attendance slumped to little more than sixty percent. The reason seemed to be that the audiences came to see the Young Elvis and his abdominal muscles, not the old druggy with the paunch.

The other show stopper was the Elvis Estate, who refused to allow any original music in the show. No moving the plot ahead with a new creation. Every number had to be one that Mr. Presley himself had performed. If you haven't got the rights, out goes the lights. Elvis left the building.

73 ANNEKENSTEIN

It's no wonder that many Islanders get pretty tired of their own island being identified as the land of *Anne of Green Gables."* There's more to this island than Anne, and I don't mean potatoes. There were a lot of objections when the face of the freckled orphan appeared on the PEI license plates.

A couple of clever young Islanders, David Moses and Rob Macdonald decided to do something about it. Along with other young comedians, male and female, they put together a satiric evening called "Annekenstein." The idea was that *"Anne of Green Gables,"* after a successful run of several years, had become a monster that was terrorizing the entire island. After a successful run of several years, I finally got to see this show, along with the Charlottetown cast of our Anne.

One of the things I remember vividly was a six foot four young man, Rob Macdonald, lying on a psychiatrist's couch and wearing one of those little straw hats with the red pigtails that little tourist girls love to buy. His helpless, hopeless identification with Anne Shirley was hilarious. There was also a group therapy session with several literary heroines which ended up, as I remember, in a bench clearing brawl. Then there was a monologue by an actress playing the part of Josie Pye who delivered a ten minute rant about her rival Anne Shirley, it was titled "That Bitch."

Perhaps the funniest scene of all was an appearance on the Ed Sullivan Show in which the entire plot, score and dances of our musical was rendered frantically in the short space of two minutes and forty seconds.

I wish it was still running during Charlottetown summers as a healthy antidote to our version.

74 THE PETERING OUT PRINCIPLE

In the late seventies, I was hosting a CBC Radio show called "Morningside," when I got a call from Alan Scales, the lawyer for the Festival, telling me of recent developments in the Charlottetown summer season-to-be.

It seems that the Festival had appointed a former CBC executive from the West Coast to guide the good ship Charlottetown. He suggested that the orchestra, the cast and the crew to be cut in half to save money. There was even an implication that the authors of *"Anne of Green Gables"* had a hell of a lot of nerve still charging royalties after so many years.

On "Morningside" I had just finished interviewing Laurence Peter the author of the book "The Peter Principle" which states that people are constantly being promoted beyond their level of competency. He confessed to me off mike after the interview that he got the idea for the book while examining the Vancouver operation of the CBC. Maybe this was what we were faced with now. When I told Norman about Alan Scales's phone call he suggested that Alan better hot foot it up here to Toronto to see if this CBC executive, not yet in charge of us all, meant what he said.

The result of the whole thing is that the steam rising from my CBC office three days later told Mr. Scales that we meant business. If the Festival went through with the idea of this former Canadian Broadcorping Castration sibilant serpent (butt out, Charlie) then the Campbells and I would pull our musical from the Festival.

I don't know where this interloper is now, but we stayed. He went back home "to from whence he came." (Guys and Dolls, Act Two, Scene One.)

75 PETE OF GREEN GABLES

Bill Hancox was a dynamite Islander who changed the calendar of Prince Edward Island. He invented a horse race called the Gold Cup and Saucer. Originally it happened in the middle of September. To get the tourists in on it, he decided to change it to the middle of August. There's a big parade with floats and a beauty contest with each girl representing a horse. Wait a minute…I meant each girl wearing the racing colors of one of the competing horses. But Islanders seem so set in their ways, that many of them still think the summer is over after the Gold Cup and Saucer Race, no matter if the temperature is boiling.

Bill was also one of those, along with Colonel Frank Storey and Frank McKinnon, who got the Festival started, but deep down in his heart there was a longing…to play Matthew Cuthbert. I don't think Peter Gzowski had a deep longing to play *"Anne of Green Gables,"* but thanks to Bill Hancox it happened.

There was going to be a fund raiser for the Festival in the off season to be held at the Delta Hotel in Charlottetown. Peter Gzowski had organized a golf tournament in connection with the evening gala in the Delta hotel. A bunch of luminaries offered to help. The Islander's own Mike Duffy and his CBC pals, Peter Mansbridge and the afore mentioned Peter Gzowski.

I couldn't attend because I was chained to my "Morningside" desk, but Bill Hancox asked me to contribute a script based on our musical. The result was "Pete Of Green Gables," a fifteen minute sketch with Bill Hancox at last as Matthew, Catherine McKinnon as a feisty Marilla, Peter Mansbridge as the narrator, Cynthia Dale as a nympho-maniacal Diana Barry with designs on Peter, and Mike Duffy as the town gossip Rachel Lynde. I would have given anything to see Mike in Rachel Lynde's bonnet and apron.

The whole thing was done as a radio show sponsored by the makers of

SHINE, "the Island drink with a difference, refreshingly provocative and at the same time completely numbing to your senses."

Norman Campbell mouthed all the sound effects. From the opening; seagulls by flapping a two dollar bill; the Island being swept by the sea, a long, loud snore; then a train whistle, penny-type followed by shunting (heavy breathing). He also created the sound effect of corks being pulled from bottles, added a few glug-glugs, a hiccup and a belch. Not bad for a tee-totaller.

I know that "Pete" of Green Gables handled himself well when he said to Bill Hancox's Matthew "Good Morningside. I was beginning to be afraid you weren't coming for me. I know that Islanders like to take their time, but holy cow, this has been ridiculous. See that cherry tree down there? Do you know what I was going to do if you hadn't come for me? I would go down to that big wild cherry tree and practice chip shots all night."

(NORMAN CAMPBELL EFFECT OF HITTING A GOLF BALL).

> PETE: Am I talking too much? People who write to the CBC are always telling me I am. Patrick Watson says my tongue must be hung in the middle it flaps so.
> MATTHEW: Actually I came down to the station to pick up a girl.
> PETE: Oh what fun! I like girls. Can we do it together?
> MATTHEW: I'll let Marilla do it.
> PETE: Does Marilla like to pick up girls too?
> MATTHEW: Never mind. I'll carry your bag.
> PETE: Oh I can caddy it. It's an excruciatingly old bag. Thank goodness I'll never have to use it again after I win the tournament to-morrow.

(LOTS OF COCOANUT SHELLS WHILE NORMAN DOES THE MOUTH PART OF THE HORSE.}

> PETE: (SINGS) *Once I thought I'd like to be,*
> *A Sunday pundit, CTV,*
> *White and pink and lazy as can be,*
> *But I'd be gone while summer's on,*
> *So now I think it over*
> *Gee, I'm glad I'm no one else but Pete.*

It goes on to the end, but I CAN'T FIND THE WORDS of the rest of the script.

76 ANNE OF GREEK GABLES

That's what we called Tracy Michailidis's Anne for three years, 1994—96.

And then she turned around and became "Emily of New Moon," Richard Ouzounian and Marek Norman's musical version of Lucy Maud's novel, a fictional treatment about her own desire to be a writer. This musical lasted only two seasons. I told Marek Norman why I thought it had such a short life on the Charlottetown stage: "It's the same plot as Anne, there are superficial differences, but there is the same strict guardian, the same Diana-like best friend, the same irresponsible male teacher."

Casting Tracy in the role of Emily, when she had played Anne the previous seasons only pointed up the similarities in the two stories. The television series of the same name managed to mask those differences more effectively.

Anyway, back to Tracy of Greek Gables. She was a highly intelligent young lady and when Marilla told her to "Fetch some sticks for the fire, not big sticks mind" Tracy went backstage where prop master Paul Smitz had a little puzzle waiting for her. He had arranged the sticks in a word, not easy to recognize and despite the fact that she had only a few seconds, she recognized the word nine times out of ten.

77 BACKSTAGE GAMES

One of the wondrous sights backstage had to be Lorraine Foreman skating up and down the long hallways before the show, during intermission or during rehearsals. She was never one to waste time sitting around doing nothing.

Heidi Ford, one of the bubbliest of all the Dianas, claims that the backstage crew would play harmless tricks on her during the cordial drinking drunk scene. The cordial was usually water and food coloring or, if you were lucky, cranberry juice. But sometimes one of the stage hands would plop in a strawberry that had been marinating in liquid since the morning and was by now all shredded and stringy like some unknown marine animal.

Chilina Kennedy recalls the 'Bear story'.

"In 2000, the first year I played Anne, I shared a dressing room with Raquel Duffy. That season the Festival was presenting *"Anne of Green Gables"* as well as the second year of "Emily." Trish Lindström, who played Emily, occupied the room adjoining ours. We had a lot of laughs that summer, which included a white stuffed bunny making his way into the pageant scene night after night, someone peeing their pants onstage from laughing and the assistant-director breaking into my house to rearrange my furniture in the middle of the night.

However the story I remember best is the case of the missing bear. Di Nyland-Proctor, who directed *"Anne of Green Gables"* for a few years, gave me a lovely stuffed teddy bear for opening night, which I kept in my dressing room and loved very much. I used to talk to him like he was my friend during the shows....until one day, he went missing. I came offstage during a break and found him...gone. I couldn't figure out whether he's been stolen or lost and Anne with an "e" was pretty upset. I could only imagine how the Bear was feeling."

She continues: "my dressing roommates, Trish, Raquel and Kristin Gauthier, were very supportive, concerned and helped me look for him and comforted me through my ordeal. The next day when I came into work, I found a ransom note on the call board with a picture of my teddy bear gagged and handcuffed.

So I figured out that this was a joke and it became my job to find my bear and his captors. This game of find-the-bear became very elaborated and long-running, which most of the cast was a part of as it gathered legs. Eventually, as the daily clues progressed on the board, Bear was finally given

Chilina's Bear "Bear in Captivity"

Kristin Gauthier Raquel Duffy Trish Lindström "The Bear-Nappers"

back to me and I was shocked to hear that it had been Raquel, Kristin and Trish behind it the whole time. Everyone lived happily ever after, even if I was disillusioned.

The lesson for all actors is a simple one: NEVER trust dressing room-mates, EVER.

They will always steal you bare."

Other backstage surprises: Mrs. Blewett's bean pot. "Here, stir this" would have the strangest concoctions in it, including little plastic spiders.

"Matthew, mind the eggs" When Marilla would take them from Matthew, she exited the stage while Anne did her little plate throwing dance with the shy bachelor. Off stage, Liz Mawson as Marilla, would do a little dance too, passing the eggs to one of the stage hands, who would dance with her while putting little plastic baby chicks in among the eggs.

Often on closing night, the prop master would put lead weights in the usually lightweight bag of potatoes that Matthew carried out of Blair's store.

Another closing night ritual was the sweet revenge that occurred when Gilbert Blythe came offstage in the closing number of Act One. There was demure little Miss Anne Shirley shoving a cool whip ice cream cone right into his face.

But the most talked about closing night ritual had to do with the rumours about the famous tassel dance performed by Gail Hekala (Mrs. Blewett) in the ladies dressing room, no males allowed. They were pounding on the door trying to get in, but alas without success.

78 THE CRICKETS AGAIN

I repeat again what Alan Lund used to say "today's bad reviews are wrapped in tomorrow's fish and chips." One of the harshest reviews came in Toronto from Urjo Kareda when our musical was playing the O'Keefe Centre. Two years later he was in London for his honeymoon and he reviewed our London production. This time he loved the show, the script and the music he had previously panned, He must have had a helluva good honeymoon.

In Vancouver, the legit theatre critic passed away or moved away or just went away and his place was taken by the food critic. When our musical came to town on one of its several tours, this man, I can't remember his last name but his first name was Richard, proceeded to lambaste our efforts. A few years later I was touring with a musical version of my book "Old Charlie

Farquharson's Testament." This same Richard lambasted my efforts again.

How sweet was my revenge when at the curtain call I had the opportunity to talk to the audience about both pannings and say: "I don't know Dick, but then I don't think he does either."

79 ANNE REVISITED

One of the most successful productions of our musical was by Alex Moustakas, who is the Artistic Director of Drayton Entertainment, a successful chain of live theaters in Southern Ontario. "Not Bad," as we Canadians tend to say for a guy who started out as Anne's teacher, Mr. Phillips, in Charlottetown.

His production of our Anne opened in June 2006 at the headquarters in Drayton, Ontario, to play later on in the summer at the King's Wharf Theatre, in Penetang. Alex wisely chose Diane Nyland-Proctor as director. She was former artistic director of the Charlottetown Festival, and Josie Pye, circa 1966.

She drew cast members from former Charlottetown seasons. For her Anne, she chose Jennifer Toulmin, who had been *"Anne of Green Gables"* in the Festival for four years (2002-2005). For Matthew Diane dug a bit farther back in the PEI past and cast Doug Chamberlain. He had graduated from the role of Mr. Phillips, where he was hysterically funny, but at the time I thought he was too young to play Matthew. I was anxious to see if time had done its proper work and it most certainly had. Doug brought the spirit of Peter Mews's first Charlottetown Matthew to Drayton as well as his own priceless comedic talent.

Other valuable Charlottetown additions to the cast were Val Hawkins as Marilla and Glynis Ranney as Miss Stacy, with her new husband playing the part of the teacher, Mr. Phillips.

Glynis had been one of our Charlottetown Annes in 1991-92. I loved her novel approach to the part, in which Anne seemed to be the recreation of Sarah Bernhardt, always the actress and always on stage. Hers was a colourful addition to the Festival roster. Backstage she was also unusual, she spent hours practicing on her favorite instrument, the tuba. Recently she has been starring in musicals at the Shaw Festival.

Valerie Hawkins as Marilla, had played Mrs. Barry in PEI and understudied the perennial Liz Mawson. In Drayton and Penetang, Val did one thing that no previous Marilla had ever done before or since, something unusual. When she pulled the blankets off to reveal Anne with dyed green hair…she laughed. And so did the audience. It made Anne's woeful plight an even richer experience.

The combination of Jenny and Dougie was pure magic. I saw the opening performance at Drayton and the final one in Penetang. The bond between the two had grown even stronger. There were many tears backstage at the parting.

80 ANOTHER VISITATION

The theater in Stirling Ontario has become a second home for me. I have performed the revue "Don Harron and Friends" "Charlie Farquharson and Them Udders" (along with pianist/composer/conductor David Warrack and my Claudette), and also in what has become an annual event "The Old Mixed Bag Review" with a cast of senior performers.

But it was Caroline Smith's production of *Anne of Green Gables* that first drew me to the Stirling Festival Theatre. Caroline had been one of the dancers at Charlottetown, and had done the 1986 National Tour with Alex Moustakas as Mr. Phillips. After working for him in his theater in Drayton, Alex encouraged her to open her own theater in this little country town. He suggested Stirling because his fiancee, now Mrs. Moustakas, came from that lovely place. She has been a very successful artistic director there for the past ten years.

Blanche Lund had told me that this Stirling "Anne' was something I must see. It was playing for the second consecutive summer season. Sarah Blair Irwin, a local girl, was a winsome Anne. Lorraine Foreman was playing a strong Marilla. I had seen Lorraine many times at the Festival as Mrs. Lynde. (I should have said the other Festival. Stirling has every right to call itself a Festival, because of the variety of its fare).

Mrs. Lynde was Diane Fabian, one of my favorite "Old Mixed Baggers"

Matthew was another member of the Charlottetown cast, David Hughes, probably the shortest Matthew ever. There have been tall Matthews, like Ron Hastings and Michael Fletcher, both imposing with their strong, deep voices, but it was remarkable to have a Matthew who was the same height as Anne, and one of the very best.

Another remarkable feature was the rendering of the score by a mere duo,

Caroline Smith

Diane Fabian, Terry Doyle, Sara Blair Irwin, Lorraine Foreman "A Stirling Cast!"

keyboard and drums, (OK two and a half men. He played the xylophone on the side.)

In ten years Caroline Smith has done some amazing productions. I thought her version of the musical "Oliver" was superior to that of Stratford's, it had more heart. Her production of "Peter Pan" was based on her own adaptation of the James M. Barrie Novel. No songs but lots of flying. I learned a lot more about Wendy, played by one of our Annes, Jennifer Toulmin, than I ever had before.

Stirling Theater did a stage version of the movie "Singing In The Rain." It went well except on the opening preview, when the front row audience got drenched in the splash of the title number.

Every year around Holiday time, Caroline does a pantomime based on a fairy tale. One version is for the for the youngsters and families, and an adult rated version is for the oldsters. The X-rated version sells out lightning fast every year. Those country people love the naughty stuff, who knew! This year's production is "Goldilocks and the Three Bares." Last year's production was "Pinocchio," I'll leave it to your imagination what grew when that little wooden boy told a lie.

Caroline also did an adaptation of our musical "Anne of Green Bagels" and it was performed by her Young Company. I never saw it but she very generously gave me a copy of the script and the rights to use it as I please.

ANNE OF GREEN BAGELS
Lovingly spoofed by Caroline Smith
for the Stirling Festival Theatre Young Company Cabaret 2004

LADIES:

Six or seven times a week
We take up our position
Then we open our throats
Like some nanny goats
'Til they call the intermission

All the people of Stirling town
Are jealous of our vocals
For we love to sing
Almost anything
Like good gossip all about the locals
We love to lie about the locals

We...are...
Great voices of the stage
With soprano clear and alto deep
We rhyme everything we can rhyme
From great arias to Sondheim
We are great voices of the stage

KATE: Girls! Look! It's Matthew Cuthbert

LIVIA: Dressed in his Sunday suit!

BRIT B: And on a Tuesday!

BRIT M: Why isn't he home, having a heart attack?

MARILLA: Matthew's off to Bright River, to meet the train

LADIES:	The train?
MARILLA:	We're getting a little puppy from the pound in Nova Scotia.
AMANDA:	Well! You're never through with surprises 'til you're dead!
NATASHA:	But Marilla! You don't really know what kind of dog you'll be getting.
BRIT B:	It could be a mutt...
BRIT M:	It could have fleas...
TIFFANY & JOCELYN:	It could pee on your carpet!
MARILLA:	Don't you people have anything better to do than stand around and gossip all day?
ALL:	No!

Our meeting can continue
Now we've found out just which
Dog pound Matthew's come from...
And he's bringing home a bitch!

We are great voices of the stage
With soprano clear and alto deep...

(The Ladies leave...Anne and Matthew enter)

ANNE:	If you're looking for the 5:30 train, it's been and gone
MATTHEW:	Oh?
ANNE:	I suppose you are Mr. Matthew Cuthbert? My name is Anne Shirley.
MATTHEW:	So!
ANNE:	Do you know what I was going to do if you hadn't come for me?
MATTHEW:	No.

ANNE: I was going to run down the train tracks to that big Becker's store, see it? And I was going to hang around the Slurppy counter until they kicked me out at closing time. Wouldn't that be lovely?

MATTHEW: I guess so…

ANNE: It seems so wonderful that I'm going to live with you and belong to you.

MATTHEW: I'll let Marilla do it.

ANNE: WHAT?

MATTHEW: Nothing. Here. Let me take your bag.

ANNE: OK (*He takes it and immediately drops it on the floor*)

MATTHEW: Oh, my God! What's in there?

ANNE: My bowling ball. A set of weights, An anvil or two…why?

MATTHEW: I'm having a heart attack…

ANNE: Oh, don't be silly. We have another whole act to get through before that happens!

MATTHEW: Oh. OK…*(they quickly turn and…)*
Here we are at Green Bagels, Come on in.

MARILLA: Matthew? Why Matthew Cuthbert, who's that?

MATTHEW: Hmmm?

MARILLA: Where's the female puppy?

MATTHEW: Well, there wasn't any female puppy.
There was only…her.

MARILLA: Well, this sucks.

ANNE: You don't want me. You don't want me because I'm not a bitch. Oh, I might have known it!

(Howls. Matthew has a heart attack.)

MARILLA: Not stop that! You've gone and given Matthew a heart attack. That's the fifth one this week.
             Now, what's your name?

ANNE: Would you call me Britney?

MARILLA: Call you Britney! Is that your name?

ANNE: Well, it's not exactly my name. But whenever I'm in dire anguish, I have always imagined that I'm Britney Spears

             (*sings a Britney hit*).

MARILLA: Stop that! All right...whatever your name is. Let's go and find out how this mistake occurred...
             (*Mrs. Spencer enters.*)
             Mrs. Spencer! We sent word through your brother Robert to bring us a puppy. And look what we got!

SPENCER: (*Giggles*) Oh isn't this a funny predicament!

MARILLA: The thing to do now is set it straight.

SPENCER: Mrs. Peter Blewitt. The very thing! I don't think we'll have to send the child back to the dog pound after all. You come along with me. As I always say "Two Wongs in a Shanghai phone book don't make a Wright!

             (*Mrs. Blewitt enters. She is 15 months pregnant*).

             Hello! Mrs. Blewitt, may I introduce you to my friend Marilla Cuthbert and this charming orphan slave... I mean girl...

             (*off stage baby cry*)

BLEWITT: Them kids! I keep them down at the bottom of the well until puberty. All right! I'm coming down there and whale the daylights outta ya!

MARILLA: She seems nice and well adjusted

SPENCER: Oh, yes. In her spare time, she runs the Ontario Teacher's Federation.

ANNE"   *(sings some Britney Spears)*

MARILLA: Anne!

BLEWITT: We don't want no Canadian Idols 'round here! All right, come here. Let me have a look at you. Well, you're pretty skinny, but I guess you'll live a week or two. All right, Mrs. Spencer, I'll take her. How much?

MARILLA: Well, I don't know. I think I should take her home again and discuss it with my brother. If we decide NOT to keep her, I'll throw her down your well tomorrow morning. Now will that suit you Mrs. Blewitt?

BLEWITT: Well, if you're going to threaten me with subtext, delivery and innuendo like that, I guess it'll have to!

(musical transition back to Green Bagels)

MATTHEW: You're back.

MARILLA: So it would appear.

MATTHEW: I finished my heart attack and took Pearl for a tinkle. She's having her oats now. We're getting a bit low on oats…Oh, Marilla, I still think we should have…! Anne!

(They run together in slow motion, the Matthew has another heart attack)

MARILLA: Oh, look. You've gone and done it again. You start CPR and I'll get the zappers. *(Anne bashes his chest)*

MATTHEW: Wow! That's got it going again. Thanks!

ANNE: My pleasure!

LYNDE: *(Offstage)* Yoo Hoo!

MATTHEW: I know who that is…

LYNDE:	*(entering)* I saw you go by in the buggy and thought I'd come over.
MARILLA:	Come in, you nosy old bag.
LYNDE:	Well, I could tell you didn't get what you expected. Where's the puppy?
MARILLA:	Anne, this is Mrs. Lynde come to see you. Isn't that nice?
LYNDE:	Come over here child, and let me have a look at you. Well! They're never going to crown you Miss Canada, that's for certain. And did you ever see such freckles? And hair as red as carrots!
ANNE:	How dare you! How would you like such things said about you? How would you like to be told that you are an adledpated sycophant with an indeterminate intelligence quotient and a tendency to corpulence in the gluteal regions.
LYNDE:	I think I'm insulted, but I'm not sure.
MARILLA:	Anne, you will apologize to Mrs. Lynde at once.
ANNE:	I could never do that!
MARILLA:	Oh, all right. Then I'll have to send you to your room…
ANNE:	Fine.
MARILLA:	…and then Matthew will have to haul out a ladder, bring you down to the porch and sing a whole song that we have to pretend not to hear until he convinces you to apologize anyway.
MATTTHEW:	Yep. Probably give me another heart attack.
ANNE:	Oh, all right…one apology coming up *(music intro begins)*

> *Mrs. Lynde, you bag of wind*
> *You have been wronged and I have sinned*
> *But now's my chance*
> *To sing and dance*
> *And warble high like Jenny Lind*
> *I can sing loud, I can sing high*
> *I can make Teamsters sit and cry*
> *I learned these notes from a beagle hound*
> *In the orphan pound…*
> *(sing very high note, Lynde exits crying)*

MATTHEW: Good, that's got rid of her. I'll have to remember to sing those high notes next time she comes around to borrow a mickey of raspberry cordial.

MARILLA: Well, if you're going to stay here at Green Bagels, you better start going to school. Here's a note for Mr. Phillips. Anne here's someone I think you could be good friends with, sweet

Diana Barry!

DIANA: Hello Anne!

ANNE: Hello Diana! You have a perfectly lovely name. Diana is my favourite dead British Princess.

DIANA: Wow. That was awkward…Marilla, could Anne come with me to the Sunday school picnic this Saturday?

MATTHEW: Excuse me, but shouldn't a *Sunday* school picnic be on a *Sunday?*

DIANA: Who asked you?
(Matthew has a heart attack, Marilla quickly thumps his chest and he "recovers")

ANNE: Please can I go, Marilla!?

MARILLA: SURE

ANNE/DIANA: Hooray!

MATTHEW: How come we never go to picnics, Marilla?

MARILLA: Nobody's ever asked us *(Marilla and Matthew exit)*

DIANA: We can go swimming at the picnic too, Anne. Tillie Boulter nearly drowned last year!

ANNE: It must be such a romantic experience to be nearly drowned!

DIANA: Not really. She swallowed about a gallon of lake water and threw up in the in ice cream.
(Anne and Diana exit as the school kids "surf" on)

KIDS: *Think about homework? No, that sucks!*
Think about spending my back-to-school bucks!
Think about the Mall where we love to shop
Think about shopping 'til we drop!
School again! School again! School again!

AMANDA: Chill, girlfriends—it's teacher dude Phillips
(Mr. Phillips crosses)

ALL: Yo. Mr. P!

PHILLIPS: Chill, my classroom honeys.

PRISSY Hey, big spender! *(Mr. Phillips chases Prissy offstage)*

GILBERT: *(entering)* Whazzup! *(all the girls scream and swarm Gilbert)*

ANNE: Who is *that*, Diana?

DIANA: That's Gilbert Blythe, number one school stud. He's awfully handsome—and he knows it too. Everybody's crazy about him.

JOSIE: Why, Gilbert Blythe, you dirty little...!
(everyone laughs)

DIANA: ...especially that Josie Pye. *(Josie is giggling and flirting with Gilbert)*

PHILLIPS:	All right. My diminutive minions. Sit down and like… meditate.
GILBERT:	Hey, what are these? Carrots?
ANNE:	You mean hateful boy! How dare you! *(brake the slate)*
PHILLIPS:	Whoa! Serious anger issues. What's your problem, little dudette?
GILBERT:	It was all my fault Mr. P. I was like—totally hitting on her, so I guess she figured she could, like…totally hit me back.
JOSIE:	*(Gerry Springer show style)* If she want my man, she better watch her back!
GIRLS:	You said it girlfriend! *(chanting)* Josie… Josie… Josie…
PHILLIPS:	I think you two better stay and work out your karma. The rest of you, to the Mall!
ALL:	Hooray! *(almost everyone exits)*
GILBERT:	So—like—you wanna hang with me at the Saturday Sunday-School picnic or what?
ANNE:	No, Gilbert Blythe!
GILBERT:	Whatever! Hey Girls! I'm available! *(a crowd of giggling girls enters, with picnic baskets…cue music)*
ALL:	*Ice cream. Was ever a song so frivolous as Ice cream! It truly is so ridiculous that we'll scream But then we just keep on singing 'til we're through— how true!*
MINISTER:	All right! Everyone ready for the egg and spoon race?
ALL:	NO!!!
MINISTER:	Suit yourselves.

DIANA:	Anne! I think Gilbert wants to be your beau!
ANNE:	I shall hate Gilbert Blythe for the rest of my life.. or at least until the end of this show…
JOSIE:	That's good, bee-yotch, because he my man!
ANNE:	He is not!
JOSIE:	You shut yo mouth…! *(they cat fight)*
LYNDE:	It's ready!
ALL:	*Now it's frozen to the core* *Act one was getting to be a bore* *Here's the moment we've been waiting for…*Act Two!
STACEY:	Good morning, boys and girls!
GIRL:	Hey. You're not Mr. Phillips!
STACEY:	No, I'm not, Mr. Phillips won't be coming back!
ALL:	Aww!
STACEY:	He went on a spiritual journey to Tibet.
GILBERT:	I heard he had to go to Vegas with Prissy Andrews.
STACEY:	Who asked you, pretty boy. Anyway, I think we'll have our first class outside!
GIRL:	Outside?
ANNE:	But the weather report says there's a 90% chance of rain.
JOSIE:	And I have hay fever.
GILBERT:	I'm totally allergic to bee stings.
DIANA:	Can't we study something useful, like basic bookkeeping?
STACEY:	*(weeping)* No! The only thing I know how to teach is nature study…*(she exits, sobbing…everybody follows)*

MATTHEW:	Anne of Green Bagels…
ANNE:	Matthew!
MATTHEW:	Well now, what did you learn you first day at school?
ANNE:	Absolutely nothing!
MATTHEW:	That's my girl!
ANNE:	Matthew, has Marilla made me that new dress yet?
MATTHEW:	Nope. That woman has no more fashion sense than a colour blind disco queen in a polyester factory. But look here! I got you something from the General store in Carmody!
ANNE:	A new dress! Wait until Josie Pye get a load of this. But Matthew, you shouldn't have strained your heart for me…
MATTHEW:	'Tweren't nothing. Only had seven heart attacks on the way home and it was worth every one. *(Marilla enters with Diana, who is obviously drunk)*
DIANA:	*Kindred spirits…*Hello Matthew!
ANNE:	Diana!
MARILLA:	This is the fifth time I've found the girl drinking my currant wine.
DIANA:	Well, what else are you gonna do in Avonlea on a Monday night?
PRISSY:	*(entering pregnant, followed by Mr. Phillips)* I could answer that one.
SPENCER:	*(entering, followed by kids)* How about having a concert?
ANNE:	I thought you didn't know anything about nature study.

SPENCER:	Nature study…and concerts!! All right, everyone, one two three four!
ALL:	*Prince Edward Island, A dot on the map* *Far from Ontari-ario—o* *Someday we'll visit and we'll have lots of fun* *Now that we know this "Anne of Green Gables" show!*
SPENCER:	Ladies and gentlemen! I have just received word that the winner of this week's 6/49 draw is from Avonlea School. Miss Anne Shirley.
ALL:	Hooray!
MATTHEW:	Hello? I just had a heart attack over here and no one noticed!
ALL:	Sorry!
MATTHEW:	Can I have my cue again, please?
SPENCER:	Ladies and gentlemen! I have just received word that the winner of this week's 6/49 draw is from Avonlea School. Miss Anne Shirley.

(Matthew has another heart attack and this time everyone watches and applauds. Marilla takes him to his chair.)

LYNDE:	My fellow citizens! It makes me very humble *(everyone, including Mrs. Lynde, says "Aww" and exits.)*
MARILLA:	All that running around for puffed sleeves…I told you it wasn't good for your heart…
MATTHEW:	Give it a rest already, Marilla!
MARILLA:	Now you just sit here while I get the Sal Volatile.
MATTHEW:	What the hell is that?
MARILLA:	I have no idea. *(exit)*

ANNE:	Oh Matthew! What a wonderful night. All the way home I just kept thinking about the first time I saw Green Bagels. I'm so happy that you decide to keep me, even though I wasn't a puppy.
MATTHEW:	We'd rather have had you than a dozen puppies. I guess it wasn't the puppy who won the 6/49, was it?
ANNE:	No…Matthew, what's wrong?
MATTHEW:	*(obviously having a heart attack)* Just…busting proud of my little girl, that's all *(music cue)*
ANNE:	Marilla…Matthew's going to…sing, Marilla!
MATTHEW:	*Anne of Green Ba…* *(but he has a heart attack. Blackout. Lights up catches Matthew exiting. He looks at the audience, then quickly has another heart attack. Marilla and Lynde enter, stepping over the dead body)*
MARILLA:	*(music cue)* Oh, Matthew! Matthew!, You mustn't think I'm just a crotchety old maid! It's not my fault that the writers didn't give me any good song to sing or comedy to play…
	It's never been easy for me to say things but *I can't find the words…so I'll just start humming*
	Hmmmmm Hmmmmmm (etc) *I can't find the…*
ANNE:	HI!
MARILLA:	You near scared out of my growth! Where'd you skip off to?
ANNE:	Over to Doctor Malcolm's. I used my 6/49 winning to get Matthew a heart transplant. Look!
MATTHEW:	*(sitting up suddenly)* Who's your Daddy! *(Marilla and Mrs. Lynde have heart attacks and collapse)*

120

ANNE:	Oh well. You can't win them all
GILBERT:	Anne! Anne Shirley! I wish to speak with you Anne!
ANNE:	What to do you want now?
GILBERT:	Look—can't we be friends? With your money and my looks we could run this town.
ANNE:	I don't know. What do you think everyone? Should Gilbert and I be sweethearts?
ALL:	YES!!!
ANNE:	Oh all right then. Come here, you big stud muffin.
	(they start to take off their clothes and make out as the chorus enters and hides them)
CHORUS:	And they all lived happily ever after.
	(Bows)

81 ANNE OF THE OTHER ISLAND

I never got to see one of the most unusual renditions of our Island story. It was only a fifteen minute sketch at an evening devoted to Canadian musicals, a Carribean version and the island referred to was Jamaica. I would have loved to hear the calypso rhythms of the parody lyrics to our songs, featuring Dennis Simpson as Gilbert and Salome Bey as Anne, with white freckles on her cheeks. I have tried to track it down but my search for the moment is in limbo. Instead of eggs and spoons I'll bet that was an event at that other Island's picnic.

82 LONDON LIFE-LY

Just before Christmas 2007, I went to see a production of *"Anne of Green Gables"* at The Grand Theatre in London, Ontario, one of the most beautiful theaters I've ever been in. I was privileged to have played The Grand twice. The first time it was with the Famous People Players substituting for Lieutenant Governor Pauline McGibbon who said "Thanks Don, and if I

can ever pinch-hit for you as Charlie Farquharson sometime, let me know."
I replied "Can you grow stubble on your face in three days?" The second time
was with "Charlie Farquharson and Them Udders." It made me want to
come back and sit in the theater as a member of the audience. As it turned
out I had a grand evening at the Grand.

This production of *"Anne of Green Gables"* was starring Jennifer Toulmin
and Doug Chamberlain, the pair that had made such a wonderful combination in Drayton the year before.

If anything, the Drayton pairing was even better this time. Jennifer still
manages to look and act like a convincing twelve year old. Doug improves
with age, like a good bottle of wine.

Matthew's buggy was drawn by a real Pearl, not live but sufficiently two
dimensional to pull its weight. Doug did a great job of steering the buggy
which was built around a golf cart. Not according to him!

During one performance Doug accidentally killed Pearl by driving her at
breakneck speed into the wall on stage right. "Jenny and I went directly into
the first Gable scene" he said, "not knowing if I had left Steve the stagehand
bruised and torn or just gasping for life. Props came to the rescue for the next
show and I swear it was Ambrose Small, The Grand Theatre's Ghost, that
pushed my foot on the accelerator of the golf cart guiding Pearl. By the time
I had got down to my dressing room, the cast and crew had left me a PEI
breathalyzer test and a glue stick of the departed."

This is Jennifer's sixth season performing the role of Anne, having played
the part 650 times. She says: "I wears custom-made knee pads to help break
my fall from the almost constant crawling around like a child. I also wear
custom-made binders in order to make my torso appear flat, as that of an
eleven year old, until I get to grow up and wear a bra under my puffed sleeve
dress in ACT II. All my wigs and costumes are coated with fireproofing
material, because of the live flame of the candle Marilla sets in my bedroom
in Act I, scene 3. My contract specified that I must engage in extraordinary
risks in performing the role of ANNE, which includes climbing up and
down a fourteen foot ladder, performing on a platform eighteen feet high
with no barrier, aerial stunts and props landing on my face."

To complete the trio there was a new Marilla, Marcia Tratt, who had previously played Mrs. Lynde in the Grand Bend summer show. Her Marilla
was very dour, which paid off enormously in the second act finale when she

broke down and cried while expressing her love for both Matthew and Anne in the Mavor Moore lyrical song "I Can't Find the Words."

The show itself, under the direction of Susan Ferley, was a revelation. It started with the opening number when the four church ladies of Avonlea gather to have a meeting. In the lyrics they talk about their charity work, and in this production they showed what it was they were collecting. They actually produced the underwear that illustrated the lyrics "When your children get too big, we give their undies to a pygmy." I realized at this performance that this production had solved a problem that sometimes exists in that opening number. This version dispelled any vagueness about why the church ladies had gathered for their meeting as they produced from their hampers and reticules various undergarments and bits and pieces of cloth. It gave an immediate reality to the line "We send afghans to the Hindu."

The next revelation was the scene when Anne is taken to the home of the slatternly Mrs. Blewett. But this time there was no house. The scene was the Blewett's backyard, full of clothing on the line as per usual. Come to think of it, it makes sense to have all that wet clothing outside in the open air, weather permitting, of course. But the center piece of that scene consisted of an outhouse, complete with the crescent moon on the door. To complete the

Claus Andersen

Jennifer Toulmin in London four ladies, L to R. Mary Kelly, Jennifer Toulmin, Stephanie Roth, Charlotte Moore, "Welcome to our out house"

Karim Morgan, Anthony Malarky, James Quigley, Zach Smadu, Derek Paradiso, Gabriel Antonacci, Zak Kearns "The Rev and his congregation"

setting, it contained an occupant, the Blewett woman, opening the door and attempting to fix her skirt having just vacated the throne.

Here's another fresh approach. The minister was, (I believe the politically correct term is African Ontarian), played by Karim Morgan, an actor I had seen at the Stirling Festival in a revue titled "The Sixties Prime Time Variety Show." Karim was hilarious playing the judge "Heah com dee jedge," Flip Wilson's character Geraldine, and a kerchiefed Butterfly McQueen "I don't know nuthing about berthin no babies" in a recreation of the famous TV sketch Carol Burnett's take off of "Gone with the Wind."

No explanation needed or offered at the Grand. Karim as the minister added immensely to the picnic scene. No wonder. He has a list of credits as long as your proverbial arm, including the Shaw Festival, Theatre Passe Muraille, and several other productions at the Grand Theatre itself.

The school concert contained a revolutionary idea. Instead of having the Viking, the French explorer and the British invader sung by Gilbert Blythe, Diana Barry and Josie Pye, the director gave the parts to the little school children in the company. It was really refreshing to see those local youngsters strutting their stuff.

There was no curtain to hide the changing of the scene; we could see sets being moved behind a partial screen which had a lovely nineteenth century view of Prince Edward Island.

The set designer John Dinning studied illustration in Victorian children's books for inspiration. His use of birch trees as a permanent surround for all the other set designs gave it a lovely framework. The evening skies with twinkling little stars was a superb touch. Something else could be appreciated but only from the balcony, the view of the floor, the red soil on the roads and greenery of the fields.

In addition to Doug and Jenny, Charlottetown was well represented with Charlotte Moore doing her brassy Mrs. Lynde. Zak Kearns as Moody Spurgeon Macpherson, Gabriel Antonacci as Tommy Sloan, Kristin Galer as Moody's mum, Heather Shiller as Josie Pye, and they were all put through their paces by Kerry Gage, choreographic assistant to Annie Allan, and director of the Charlottetown Young Company.

Charlotte, daughter of Mavor Moore, has been in our musical seven times in five different parts. Her professional debut was as Prissy Andrews to Doug Chamberlain's Mr. Phillips. In 1995, she was Miss Stacy and Mrs. Blewett, where they gave her three days off rehearsal to get married to Patric Masurkevich, who played brilliantly a thinly disguised Conrad Black character in a mock pantomime I wrote for the 2007 Fringe Festival called "Rumpelforskin." But that's beside the point. In 2005 Charlotte was Miss Stacy and Mrs. Gillis at Stage West in Mississauga, and 2005-6 she reprised her Rachel Lynde for the Charlottetown Festival.

Charlotte was in the audience on that very first opening night back in 1965. She had just turned six and when the lady teacher started singing Charlotte's dad's song about opening windows, she turned to her mother and said "That." Her mother said "What." Little Charlotte said "I'm going to do that." Her mother replied "Oh no you're not." Opening night at Stage West in 2005 Charlotte was singing as Miss Stacy and got all choked up when she realized her own girls were in the audience, and one of them was exactly six years old. "As my mother use to say about my sister and me: one word from me and they do what they like."

Teddy Moore, Charlotte's sister, attended the closing night and this is what she e-mailed to me:

"WOW! I certainly had a very emotional time of things on Saturday.

I simply loved the show. Just loved it. And was quite overwhelmed with sadness that MM* (Norman and Elaine couldn't see it. I was also keenly aware of the gift the four of you have left behind forever and the value of such a gift. Many memories flooded back. Remember that first year? And here we are at a new incarnation all these years later. How exciting. How just. How rare. Aren't I the lucky witness!

*MM stands for Mavor Moore.

Thanks Tedde."

The rest of the Grand company held the same high standards as the Charlottetown's grads, and represented the best in Canadian theaters, with credits in Stratford, Shaw, Canadian Opera Company, Neptune Theatre, Manitoba Theatre Center. The list goes on and on and it makes for a strong national theater.

All I can say is that from my visit to the Grand Theatre that opening night is an echo of what Rachel Lynde said: "Isn't it Grand, that they got up a concert!"

83 THE VIEW FROM ST JOHN'S

John Crosbie was the wittiest, as well as one of the most acerbic members of the Federal Conservative cabinet. He is now the Lieutenant Governor of Newfoundland. It was John Crosbie who caused a storm of protest from Sheila Copps when he referred to her as "Baby" in Question Period. She replied "I'm nobody's Baby" and eventually wrote a book with the same title. John Crosbie's reply to this kerfuffle in the House at Question period was "Have a tequila, Sheila."

I had the pleasure of dining in the Crosbie home in St Johns Newfoundland in 1999, during the Year of the Older Person. Flora Macdonald and I were appointed by Health Canada as Canada's representatives. That's how I got the invite to the Crosbie home, Flora took me along. Instead of the bombastic wit I was accustomed to, I sensed that Mrs. Crosbie was the one in charge because John was meek as Mary's lamb. When we were alone together, I reminded John that he had told me a joke at a Conservative convention where I was the warm-up speaker for Joe Clark. It was during the Falklands War and John came up to me without a word of introduction and said "Did you hear that British soldiers were taking sheep back to England as war broids?"

A couple of years ago I was delighted when I heard that John Crosbie had been added to the Board of the Charlottetown Festival. I wasn't present when John saw our musical for the very first time, but I heard many reports that he emerged from the theater with his eyes streaming with tears and sobbing "Nobody told me the old fella doid."

84 LATE NIGHT AT THE MAC

A season in Charlottetown can last from May until October. Beach time is limited with an eight-show a week schedule. So its important that the resident company feel part of a family for that period of time. Esprit de corps of the acting company is terribly important for such a length of time away from home.

I had memories of the 1966 season when Jack MacAndrew organized a cabaret every night after the show.

Heidi Ford, one of the most creative performers to grace the Festival stage playing the role of Diana to Jennifer Toulmin's Anne was encouraged by director Annie Allan, and improvised a sort of high falutin society matron double-

Charlottetown Festival Archives

Heidi Ford with group of dancers "ESPRIT DE CORPS" in Liz Mawson Rehearsal

talk at their little tea party, when Diana said (in Lucy Maud's own words) "lets pretend that we're grownups and say things to each other we really don't mean." Whatever they said to each other was in mumbo-jumbo double-talk but it conveyed perfectly the relationship between two elderly society ladies.

That was only the beginning of Heidi's creativity to help bolster interest in the Festival among the children of Prince Edward Island.

I will let her explain in her own words: "We would head out to the Oak

Heidi & Kids in camp. "Camping it up"

Acres children's camp for under-privileged children in Murray River on Sunday (Day off) to visit the kids, answer questions about *"Anne of Green Gables"* from our character's point of view, and partake in an egg and spoon race or three legged race. It was a blast. The kids as part of their programming got to see Anne during the week, so they were very familiar with the play and loved to ask questions. The questions were amazing…it is incredible what they pick up on.

I did it as a favor when Danny Murphy asked me (Tim Hortons sponsors the camps) and then I did it because I loved it. All the various community events were an attempt to bridge the gap between community and the arts. I figured if they got to know us, they would want to come and share in the joy of what we do…it worked. In the meantime we raised thousands for local charities by doing a cabaret-style dinner/song in every legion hall in the back woods, and met wonderful people who came to see our shows."

A few years ago a whole cabaret was recreated by this single Charlottetown performer. Heidi's crowning achievement.

"Late Night….my baby" Heidi recalls. "I remember the first night there were eight people there, is was hard to get the machine oiled and find the right mix of songs and band and then motivating the cast…it became something magical of it's own. The cast would belt out their favorite party tunes, and band was HOT, I guess my greatest skill was in making people feel appreciated for donating their time and talents and everything else fell into place. The cast needed less from me as they gained appreciation from the roar of the crowd. Late Night was a labor of love for me."

Saturday evening show at the Mackenzie Theatre (across the road from the main theatre), took place after the regular performance. There was an admission charge of eight dollars for the general public to cover expenses, drinks and snacks were available. There usually was a line up outside the Mackenzie waiting to get in. Starting at eleven p.m. every Saturday, "Late Night at the Mac" featured casts members of the Festival doing a hastily put-together, but well organized show that was completely different every time. The band was fronted by Mike Ross, a brilliant and very hip jazz pianist whose job in Anne, ironically enough, was playing Cecil the farmer. He accompanied, various cast members doing whatever they had their hearts set on to do. There were also comic monologues, including an unforgettable one by

Heidi & Elaine. "Late Nighters"

Festival co-director Wade Lynch, confessing his pre-teenage obsession with Barbie dolls. The role of M.C. could be any one of a number of people. Heidi often performed this function. Mike Ross is now with the "Soulpepper Theatre Company" in Toronto.

One night in 2004 when Elaine Campbell and I were present, the young master of ceremonies for the evening paid us a startling compliment. *"Do you realize if these two people here tonight hadn't done what they did that none of us would be here in Charlottetown?"*

But the most important thing that came out of those once a week late nights was a strong sense of esprit de corps (french for community spirit) among the members of the Festival company.

It all started in the mind and heart of one little wisp of a thing…Heidi Ford.

In 2007 she brought something very special to the Summerside Jubilee Theatre.

"That Dance Show" a sixty-five minute presentation. Jack MacAndrew was sitting beside me on opening night and he could hardly contain his excitement, sitting on the edge of his seat with a grin from ear to ear. The headline in his newspaper column "Something wonderful is happening in Summerside," was the same quote that described the opening of *"Anne of Green Gables"* by Nathan Cohen so many years ago. It was well deserved too. What talent and energy was on that stage. Heidi had combined the cast members of "Anne and Gilbert" with ten amazing Island kids. The closing high-stepping heart-stomping number with everybody step-dancing in unison brought the house to it's feet. I would defy anyone to tell the professional dancers from the kids. The only drawback…the show was too short.

Maybe next year Heidi, with an intermission?

85 THE FRICTION OF FICTION

One of the things that many visitors to Prince Edward Island can't seem to get through their heads is that *"Anne of Green Gables"* never existed. She is a fictional character invented by Lucy Maud Montgomery when she saw a newspaper article about an orphan girl who was sent to a home somewhere in the Maritimes when they had been expecting a boy. That's it.

From that clipping Lucy Maud turned its brief report into a novel that has lasted for a hundred years and still going strong. Part of the fiction problem is that for years there has been a Green Gables house on the grounds of the Green Gables golf course. It has all kinds of knick-knacks in it, like a portrait done in human hair. It would lead the unsuspecting tourist to think that a real person actually lived there. That little house used to be the pro shop. Does that make you teed off?

Our wonderful Cape Breton comedian, Ron James, whose hilarious routines are full of what I would call blue-collar poetry, talked about this shock when he was told in that former pro shop that Anne never lived there because she was fictitious. Ron pretended to be outraged. He told the tourist guide that he was going to rent a place on the island and call it Spiderman's cottage.

86 PEARL

Perhaps the most significant contribution I made to the musical *"Anne of Green Gables"* was to give a name to Matthew's horse. I worked with Pearl, an actual horse. It was the summer of '42 (not at all like the lucky lad in the Hollywood movie who got seduced by a suddenly-widowed young bride who had just lost her husband in the war) and Pearl was twenty seven years old, an age when a horse should be put to pasture. But war is war, and it was hell for Pearl as she pulled my plow with a lot of heavy breathing. I became the slowest plowman in Canada but it was all out of sympathy for this dear horse. I never cracked the reins over her aged flanks.

When I worked on the first adaptation of Anne I was determined to immortalize my old equine friend. The line "I've just watered Pearl, she's having her oats now" became a by-word backstage and the cult of Pearl eventually blossomed onstage.

In the store scene, when Matthew makes his entrance in Blair's store to buy the dress with puffed sleeves, Cecil the farmer and Earl the mailman are already there and while Matthew was puff-puffing his inability to say puffed sleeves they used the time to swap remarks about Pearl, obviously waiting outside the store. While the audience was watching Lucilla flirting with poor Matthew, the other actors on stage were exchanging scurrilous and even scatological references about horses asses. The Pearl tradition however was only possible in the days of mikes on the floor downstage. Now that everybody seems to have one sticking out of their ear, or goodness know where, scurrilous adlibs in praise of Pearl have sadly been silenced.

My naming of Pearl became incontrovertible evidence to confront a would-be playwright (who shall be nameless, for ever and ever I hope). This person did an alternate adaptation of the novel, claiming that she had never poached on my version of the tale. However the evidence was obvious that she did, because in her purloined version the name of Matthew's horse was Pearl. Case closed. Court dismissed.

87 MID-WESTERN APPROACHES

Theatre Midwest in the USA is a conglomeration of outdoor theaters all of which average about sixty five hundred seats. It was headed by Henry Moran, who is now in Washington as the son of a Bush's Cultural czar. At one time he was located in Kansas City where he was closely connected with the Muni Opera house, which did summer musicals like "Camelot" and "Kiss Me Kate" starring Robert Goulet, with great box office success.

Norman, Elaine and I were flattered when Mr. Moran approached us with an offer, but we had difficulty conceiving our musical in front of an audience of thousands of people. Monetary greed needs no bounds, so we set up meetings with our representative (and my personal manager) Paul Simmons.

The meeting took place in Paul's office in Toronto. It was then agreed that the show would open first in Kansas City and the other theater owners could come and give our piece the once-over. It was also agreed that the producer and the director would come to Charlottetown and view the Festival production. This happened in the late summer with a view to presenting the show in the Mid-Western chain of theaters the following summer.

Following their viewing of the original Festival production there was a breakfast meeting the next morning at the Delta Hotel in Charlottetown.

The first remark out of the producer's mouth was not promising. "Well, it was pretty good but we can do it better." When we raised our concerns about playing in such a large space, the director spoke up "We'll have to cut the opening two numbers and go straight to the little broad sitting on her suitcase in the station."

I looked at Norman. Dark clouds were accumulating on the horizon and a storm was soon approaching.

The director went on "We'll have a real horse, of course. Oh by the way, we can't have that girl getting pregnant by the teacher. There's a woman out in Seattle who's been fooling around with a fourteen year old boy who claims he wants to marry her. We want none of that in our show. And we'll have to cut the drunk scene with those two little girls. That'll never go where we come from."

The pressure was building and it was ready to burst when the producer added "We'll do a dress rehearsal at the Muni Opera in Kansas City and we'll invite all the other theater owners to see it so they can critique the production."

"What do you mean by critique?" said a somewhat controlled Norman.

"Yeah, you know, throw in their two cents worth about what they think will work in your show and what won't" came the reply.

Well...the tsunami hit. I sat there like a bump on a log while a very offended Norman Campbell went into his Jesus-with-the-money-changers-in-the-temple bit.

I'll spare you the details of the stormy outpouring but it concerned their tampering with a tried and true tested and proven vehicle that had functioned well for more than thirty five years. The breakfast ended with us paying the bill and the Mid-Westerners heading for the Charlottetown Airport.

I guess we'll never play Washington's Kennedy Center now.

88 THERE IS A NEW HAVEN

A couple of years ago the Charlottetown Festival did manage to make a brief incursion into the Benighted States! a one week engagement at the Shubert Theatre in New Haven, Connecticut, the home of Yale University. The Shubert is probably the American theater's most prestigious pre-Broadway house. This is where the New York bound shows do their last cutting, carping and honing.

Anne was not Broadway bound. We learned long ago it's not that kind of show. *"Anne of Green Gables"* is not "Annie." Elaine and I didn't mind that at all. I didn't see our show at the Shubert but Elaine did. She said the sophisticated Yaleys in the audience really seemed to enjoy it, and she sent me a copy of the reviews.

New Haven critics must be as theater hardened as the Broadway bunch, but their comments were all entirely favorable...except...they all felt the show was too long.

This is understandable. By the time the school pageant comes along at the two and half hour mark, including intermission, with it's joke about the Fathers of Confederation, a digest of Canadian history, and a marching song called *"Prince Edward Island the heart of the world,"* any American theatergoer already sated with enjoyment, is ready to call it quits.

If we ever do it again on their soil our musical is going to have to be shorter. The above topics mentioned in the concert scene may be the unkindest cuts of all to Canadians, but in a foreign land, even an English speaking one, it makes sense. After all, we sure aren't gonna cut Matthew singing the title song and then slumping in his rocking chair. Better that Sir John A. Macdonald and his old boys get to walk the Yankee plank.

I wasn't there. For a more accurate perspective I defer to Wade Lynch, star of the massive Mackenzie Theater hit, "Shear Madness," and who appeared in New Haven as the teacher Mr. Philips. Here is his account of the event.

ANNE OF THE RED LIGHT DISTRICT?

"Isn't it astounding how some people communicate? With all the cultures and languages in the world, it's a wonder that people on this planet are able to relay information to each other at all. How do we, for example, explain the wonders of taffy-pulling to a fellow traveler on a train in Spain? Can the intricacies of the sport of curling be justly translated to a cheese merchant in Pauillac, Bordeaux? (Comment dit-on "hurry-hard"?) But as often as languages fail in accurately describing cultural variations, it's equally astounding how often non-verbal communication succeeds in communicating global concepts."

"For example, an index finger pressed against pursed lips means "Shhh! Be quiet!" in any language. The outlined image of a martini glass will indicate that an alcoholic beverage is available to a thirsty wanderer whether you're walking New York's 42nd Street or the Road to Morocco! And as I have learned, any building illuminated with a red light has come to mean "Love for Sale" whether you're in Anchorage, Amsterdam or Avonlea."

"In 2005 the Charlottetown Festival Company was thrilled to be touring *ANNE OF GREEN GABLES*" to the Shubert Theater in New Haven, Connecticut. The Shubert is famous as one of the important "feeder" houses where Broadway shows go for their out-of-town trials. The company, complete with cast, crew and select musicians arrived at the Shubert on a very short, very intense schedule. We had to get the show in and rehearse in under two days. While we traveled with most of the cast from the summer production, many musicians and smaller roles had to be rehearsed using local artists. We also need to ensure that our sound, lighting and technical considerations were properly addressed and rehearsed."

"The Shubert has a seasoned team of exceptional theater technicians who, while genuinely friendly and welcoming, are for the most part, strictly business, very serious about their work, and very protective of their theater. They are seasoned vets who know how to get a show up-and-open in short order and with little fanfare. With thousands of Broadway musicals under their collective belt, the "*Anne*" company was more than a little curious as to how our show would be received by a crew that had hosted the first performances of everything from "SOUTH PACIFIC "to "SWEENEY TODD." We were all a little intimidated."

"As seems always to occur in these situations, we hit a technical snag early-on in rehearsals that snow-balled as the day progressed. With the technical team on cherry pickers on stage, the company of actors had to rehearse in the house while the "new" orchestra stayed in the pit. When lights needed to be re-hung in the house, the acting company had to move into the lobby to continue our work-through without benefit of musicians. The day concluded and it was obvious that we were not going to get a full, onstage rehearsal in before the show opened. No one really panicked because the Festival company, with 40 years of "*Anne*" performances to its credit, knew that we could pretty well pull the show off under any conditions, and we had great confidence in the abilities of our hosts at the Shubert. Nonetheless, it's always risky to perform a new show in a new space without a complete run-through."

"Some of the appeal of performing "*Anne*" in a new venue for a new audience with a new crew was the opportunity to witness the reaction to the production from first-timers. At home in Charlottetown, every element of the play and the performances is familiar. Our audiences at the Confederation Center typically know every line of text, note of music and whistle-jump intimately. We were looking forward to seeing how the show would measure up with a new audience and crew. How familiar would they be with the story? Would the audience be as captivated by the spirit of PEI's famous red-head as the legions of her fans were at home? Would the seasoned crew pay attention to, or even care about the show?"

"I was playing the role of Mr. Philips, the School Master, whose interest in his pupils begins and ends with the comely Prissy Andrews. After the overture I wasn't needed on stage again until Act One Scene Ten. However, as I was also understudying the role of Matthew (which that season was being played by the terrific Michael Fletcher), I wanted to watch as much of the performance as possible. The move-in to the new space required some blocking and sight-line adjustments. I needed to observe the changes and I wanted to listen to the audience and the crew's reactions to the show."

"The overture concluded and I moved to a pre-authorized position, Stage Left, where the onstage action could be observed without interfering with the crew. I was placed shoulder-to-shoulder with a senior member of the Shubert crew; a big sturdy fellow who said little and whose stony stare gave no indication of his opinion of our show one way or the other. The first scene went very well. The tone of the play was flawlessly set by the ladies of Avonlea who sang their own virtues as "Great Workers for the Cause."

"The audience response was encouraging, enthusiastic clapping and a wave of knowing chuckles. They got it. My wing-mate techie however was unmoved.

His countenance never changed. He responded to instructions over his head-set with single syllables and passionless grunts. "Jaded," I thought. "

"Scene 2. One of my favorites, came next. Anne meets Matthew at the train station at Bright River and absolutely charms his aging heart with "Gee,. I'm Glad I'm No One Else But Me." As Anne Shirley, Jennifer Toulmin was magnificent. She sang the song brilliantly and had the Shubert audience eating out of her hand. She owned them! My new friend in the wings, however, continued unmoved and grunting as before."

"The next scene is crucial to the play and key to Anne's journey. After a long buggy ride from Bright River, Anne sees Green Gables for the first time, and falls in love with its pastoral splendor. What is supposed to happen is that after Anne and Matthew have completed their downstage cross in front of the curtain, they exit the scene Stage Right, and the lights fade to black. When they re-enter, the lights come up again, the curtain rises, and Green Gables is revealed, bathed in its late spring brilliance! It's an early June afternoon on Prince Edward Island! The skies are blue! The cherry tree is ablaze in pink blossoms and Green Gables is lit with the kind of sun that occurs only on PEI, reflected off the Atlantic and filtered through a salty breeze! That is what is supposed to happen."

"What really happened that night in New Haven, however, was drastically different. "

"As "Gee, I'm Glad " faded from the pit, the jaunty traditional music began, the curtain rose, the lights came up and......Green

Gables became bathed in a colour that could only be described as blood red! The gleaming white clapboards of the Cuthbert home were awash in a cranberry veneer, and the famed gables had transited from Emerald green to Ruby red. Whatever technical glitch had prevented us from rehearsing onstage had now been made evident on the famed stage of the Shubert Theatre. Green Gables was rose red!

In the house, the audience gasped! Onstage, Matthew, uncharacteristically, chortled! And in the wings my formerly unmoved wing-mate was aghast!

He blanched, his jaw dropped and without a moment's hesitation he cried out:

"Holy Shit! Look at that red light! Green Gables is some kinda whore-house and that old bugger's gonna pimp out that little girl!"

"It's refreshing to witness how our cherished "*Anne*" might be perceived by the unsullied perspective of a foreign viewer.

Yours respectfully,
Wade Lynch.

89 BEHIND THE FENCE AND OTHER PLACES

The fence that appears at the opening of Act II is a movable object that is held in place by two stage hands and a rope. It comes off stage at a clip and sometimes fencing accidents happen.

One of the stagehands, Garney Gallant, coming off stage with the fence, hit his head on a cement platform offstage, and passed out cold. For the rest of the season Garney's temporary resting place was marked with a chalk outline; you know the kind they use for murder victims on TV police shows!

There are other dangers too. When Gilbert Blythe and the other schoolboys get ready to take their shoes off for the "Who Wants To Put Your Shoes On" dance, they first throw their books over the fence. The stagehands are too busy holding on to that fence to defend themselves from this onslaught. Consequently the two kindred spirits, Anne and Diana, are the only ones behind that fence able to catch the books as they career over at a fair rate of speed. The big burly stagehands appreciate the fact that they are protected from violence by two little girls.

Beyond the fence, the cast found plenty of time and places to play. Our perennial correspondent Denise Fergusson takes us there:

Garney's annual Strawberry Social at a matinee intermission once a year

The Ladies of Avonlea's barbecue for the crew

Girls night out (Thursday)

Sarong Days (once a week)

The Bottle Drive (went on all summer for charity)

Matinee Bake Sales Backstage, with resultant cookbook

Crew Calendar

Avonlea Secret Lingerie Catalogue

Pajama parties with Ladies of Avonlea at Rice Point

Liz & Fen flying kites at Rice Point

Contest as to whether Garney or Glenda made the best muffins

(Votes from the cast)

We were always raising money for something.

At Rice Point, orchestra picnics, crew picnics and company picnics, with egg and spoon races, wheelbarrow races, sack races, kissing booths (all proceeds went to the heart Fund.)

Bon-fire on the beach

Yeah, memories are made of all this. It was so much FUN!!!

"The magic of coming to the Island on that ferry with the old timers, finding tears at the first sight of those red cliffs, and feeling teary as they receded on the trip back home."

Liz & Denise. "The Dolly Sisters"

Denise, Norman & Liz.
"Norman Campbell submits to a three way"

90 DRESS CODE

Curtis Barlow was an experienced Canadian government diplomat and when he was in charge of the Festival he insisted on a certain protocol for Royal Visits. When Her Majesty's youngest son, Prince Edward, made a visit to Charlottetown with his new bride, Princess Sophie, the call went out that the dress code for the evening performance was to be black tie.

Crew chief Roddy Diamond asked if that applied backstage as well. Curtis suggested that they dress decently, maybe not black tie but anything decently suitable they would wear on a social occasion, just as long as they didn't appear in Hawaiian shirts.

The boys went right out to Henderson and Cudmore and every single one of them bought themselves Hawaiian shirts. At the Royal post-show reception it made the backstage area look like a luau.

Prince Edward, Elizabeth Mawson, Leisa Way, Leon Pownal.
"Prince Edward on His Island"

Charlottetown Festival Archives

91 THE GREEN WIG CAPER AND OTHER MYSTERIES

Anne's green hair wig is a constant challenge.

Gracie Finley was hanging onto the wig for dear life under the blanket, when she felt a kick. "I was pregnant with Michael and it was the first time I felt a kick, I wanted to fling the blanket and announce to the whole theatre that my baby had kicked. Liz Mawson threw the cover back and must have wondered what was going on, I was dancing about the bedroom. I did remember to say my lines. By the way, Liz is Michael's godmother."

Malory Spiller lost hers when the cover was pulled off by Marilla to reveal Mallory's own hair. No record remains of the frantic ad-libbing that followed.

Jenny Toulmin said that she wears approximately fifty hair pins, a sewn-together headband and a red stocking cap (made from a nylon) on her head in order to survive the four wigs worn during the show.

The wig is usually well hidden backstage, both before and after its use. One night after the show, it went missing. Searching high and low to no avail. A hasty substitute had to be provided by wig mistress, Honey Landry. Some days later crewman Rich Wilson was driving on University avenue when he saw a young couple strolling along and one of them was wearing Anne's green wig. Rich followed them with his car as best he could, but he lost them. He persisted in his search and later found the wig stuffed into a garbage can. Backstage visits were stricter after this incident.

Props get lost during performances but usually there is an immediate concentrated effort to find them. Once in a while they can't be found. The Eskimo parka in the school pageant once got swept up into the flies by a stray hook on a pipe extension and went missing. The result: a topless Inuit onstage voluntarily doing a lot of the required shivering. Such so-called forgetfulness was labeled by the crew as Annezheimers.

When Alan Lund did his post-Charlottetown revival of *"Anne of Green Gables"* at the Elgin Theatre in Toronto, the first thing he did was hire Barbara Hamilton as Marilla. The sets were more elaborate than at the Festival and the Green Gables house moved in and out like the Queen Mary docking at Southampton. In one performance, something got in the way of the movement of that set and it took some time getting it onstage. Just back from Mrs. Blewett house, Barbara stood there unperturbed, and in her best Spring Thaw improv mode said to Anne, much to the amusement of the audience, "we'll just wait here until the house arrives."

92 LONG RUNS

I mentioned earlier in this book the long association Glenda Landry has with the Festival, thirty eight years and we're counting on her to continue. But she is by no means the grand champion of longevity. That position is held by Fen the Watkin man, who clocked in more than forty years, starting as the rehearsal pianist in the first season and conductor for the orchestra until a couple of years ago.

Charlottetown's perennial grand young man reluctantly announced his resignation and handed the reins over to Donald Fraser, a youthful stripling.

Fen lied about the retiring bit. First thing he did was to get involved with a radical production of our musical in 2002 in the Kitchener-Waterloo in The Center in the Square Theatre. Fen said the setup was different from what he had been used to. The stage was completely in the round, they used a multi-level, all-purpose set of ramps and stairways. There was a cast of seventy actors, all the costumes were off white, and at times adding something over them for another scene. The cast would freeze in place in a dim light while a scene was performed in the lit area. When Matthew died he was hoisted up on the shoulders of the male dancers, rather like Prince Hamlet being raised aloft at Elsinore castle on the orders of Fortinbras.

At eighty-five, Fen has recently completed six weeks of rehearsal and a performance run with another musical in the Kitchener area. I see him often at other theatrical events. He looks like a kid of seventy. Fen's favorite anecdote happened after a school matinee of *"Anne of Green Gables"* in Winnipeg. Doug Chamberlain was playing Matthew and a young boy came to see him after the show. He had played Matthew in a school production and he wanted Doug to know that when he came out for his curtain call, he was wearing angel wings.

Fen Watkin & Duncan McIntosh.
"Wigging out"

A Festival perennial is Hank Stinson, our local Charlottetown actor who became the Festival's utility man. As Denise Fergusson says "Hank has played every part in this show, except Anne and Marilla. He made a lovely gentle Matthew, and has been seen as the mailman, the farmer, the minister and many various roles in the other musicals.

He also set pen to paper and did a stage version of Lucy Maud's late novel, "The Blue Castle." It takes place in Muskoka, and has a lot of the Ontario charm of Stephen Leacock's "Sunshine Sketches of a Little Town." "The Blue Castle" premiered at Orwell Corner about six years ago and was done in the fall of 2007 by a local Charlottetown theatre company. Hank Stinson is still a man for all Charlottetown seasons. He and his wife Rowena toured Japan in 1991. She played Mrs. Barry and he played the stationmaster and understudied Matthew.

Another long time record holding belongs to Elizabeth Mawson in playing the part of Marilla. A Festival favourite, she began as a very elegant Mrs. Barry before she took over the leading role of Marilla for twenty-six seasons. Theatergoers will remember her outstanding rendition of "I Can't Find The Words" and many other contributions she made to other musicals, like "Johnny Belinda."

Denise Fergusson remembers her this way: "She always had that wonderful reserve, but my goodness, when she got with me we could be up to a all kinds of foolishness—we shared a wicked sense of humour and great giggles. I will always remember her in the Annual Maud Whitmore Concert, wearing that skin-tight red jumpsuit near the end of her "reign." She found it in a drawer and brought it to Charlottetown to show Glenda and I (it was from the old "dishy" days). We dared her to wear it in the Maud Concert and so she did and performed the funniest, sexiest number for years and knocked everyone's socks off. Afterwards when the young chorus people were all over her in awe, she just had that sly smile and called everyone "dear" (she told me she never bothered learning their names because they'd only change next year). She said, "it's kind of like Chinese food, you can't remember an hour later what you had for dinner." She just knew them all by their costumes/characters.

Perhaps, not so long a tenure belongs to the original stage Matthew, Peter Mews who created the role in 1965 and made it his own with his amusing additions. He found a pair of boots that squeaked with every step, so when he tried to sneak up the stairs to see Anne, after hurling her insults at Rachel

Lynde, Marilla has no trouble catching him in mid flight. Unfortunately those boots got lost after one of the summer seasons. Peter's upward climb never squeaked again. But he made up for it by a sly knowing look on his face when Marilla complained about "school concerts being so foolish, letting young people stay up when they'd all be better off in bed." Peter's single-entendre look after that remark put audiences in hysterics.

There were several years when Peter was away from the Festival, but I don't think it was his wish. His eventual return coincided with that of Gracie Finley's in 1984, and it was a joyous reunion. Unfortunately Peter never finished the 1985 season. Cancer claimed him and he died shortly after he had been forced to relinquish the role.

I was lucky enough to have shared the stage many times with him in productions of the New Play Society, the first season of the Stratford Festival, and several "Spring Thaws," including several ballet spoofs with which Peter brought the house down.

But I still think that Peter might agree with me that the role of Matthew Cuthbert was his finest hour on stage. And sadly, his last.

93 MUSIC WITHOUT WORDS

Arnold Spohr, director of the Royal Winnipeg Ballet, expressed a desire to do a ballet version of our musical. Naturally a new version of the score was required. Norman had the inspired idea of contacting Bob Farnon to do it. Older Canadians may remember him as one of the original cast members of that radio classic "The Happy Gang." Along with pianist-vocalist Bert Pearl, organist Kathleen Stokes, violinist Blaine Mathé, accordionist Eddie Allan, announcer Herb May, later Hugh Barlett, Bob played trumpet and was the source of much of the humour in the most popular radio show of the thirties and forties. Bob Farnon left the show to take up duties with the Canadian Armed Forces Band. After the war, Bob didn't return to Canada but was living on one of the Channel Islands (it was either Jersey, Guernsey, Alderney or Sark) probably to avoid taxation.

I don't know where or when Bob saw our musical, maybe during the London run, but he did the most marvelous film-like arrangement, which became the score for The Royal Winnipeg ballet of *"Anne of Green Gables."* I never saw the results, but listening to a recording of the music, it sounded to me like the ideal opening of a major feature film of our Anne. Since none of the lyrics were used I had no involvement with this enterprise. Yet, when the royalties were paid out, Norman insisted that I share with him, half and half. Just another example of our composer's generous nature.

Another Canadian music legend is Howard Cable. At eighty-six he bounces around this country from concert to concert like a young sprout in his twenties. He takes with him a Suite of Maritime music which includes several selections from our musical. Again no words. Howard originally arranged Norman's music for the Hanneford Silver Brass Band, but it is readily adaptable for symphony orchestras.

Howard never got involved with our stage musical, but he did do several shows for Charlottetown, including Alan Lund's "Swing" and "Singin' and Dancin' tonite."

Howard Cable is the only person I know who was mugged in downtown Charlottetown. He came out of the stage door after a late night session with the score of "Singin and Dancin" and was almost immediately set upon by an inebriated felon who proceeded to separate him from his wallet. Howard returned to his rented room on Queen Street and contacted the police about the incident. They soon tracked down the drunken thief and returned Howard's wallet to him, minus the price of a few beers. I still think this mugging belongs in the Guiness Book of Records.

94 DEPARTMENTALIZING ANNE

In 1990 Walter Learning took four Charlottetown actors with him to Japan; Elizabeth Mawson (Marilla) Ron Hastings (Matthew) Leisa Way (Anne) and Glenda Landry (Diana). Max Reimer went along to manage things. They did an hour-long version of our musical four times a day in what has become known as The Mini-Anne Department Store Tour. It was sponsored by a Japanese Company called Keio.

Leisa Way, who has been to Japan five different times, describes one dinner party held by their Japanese sponsors. "We had, of course, been briefed about Japanese social etiquette: never blow your nose at the table, leave and go somewhere private and then come back to the table. And eat whatever is placed in front of you at dinner. It is rude not to like your food…so push it around your plate and make it look like you ate some of it."

"Japanese men may pull out a chair for a woman nowadays, but back in 1990, a man's chair was pulled out for him, but not for a woman's. There were no other women but Glenda, Liz and I. I will never forget the look on Glenda's face when the men pulled out chairs for all the other men at the table, and left the three of us standing there while they sat down. Glenda was just a bit miffed!"

"Glenda had been strategically placed beside the Big Wig, because we knew that: number one, Glenda could talk to anyone and make them laugh, and number two, this Big Wig had mentioned that Glenda reminded him of a Japanese lady with her size and coloring."

"Needless to say, sitting our Glenda beside the one guy we needed to schmooze was a brilliant move, because despite the language barrier she had him laughing within minutes. That is, until the raw octopus showed up…stunningly displayed on a platter."

"I was a small town girl from Northern Ontario. The thought of eating fish raw had never ever entered my mind, let alone eating octopus or any squishy delights. For example, the fishermen from Japan regularly unload a net full of larvae. The larvae are the young of a kind of water insect. Many water insect larvae are eaten in Japan. Ooey gooey! The three of us looked at each other. Then we looked at Walter, then back to each other, remembering the words of wisdom…never refuse anything on your plate that they have specially prepared for you."

The Big Wig said: "'Who will try first?' Very bravely, in a meek voice I might add, Glenda said: "I" (gulp) will.' Glenda, knew full well that her job was to help seal this deal. And the deal was that these Big Wigs would sponsor a tour of Japan with the whole company the following year. We watched the humungus tray of squiggly raw octopus passed around the table. When it reached Glenda, her face seemed to turn a little paler as she looked at it. When it was placed in front of her, the Big Wig grabbed his chopsticks and secured a rather large piece and brought the entire piece up to Glenda's mouth. She grimaced and bit down on the end of the octopus leg. And the rest of the story is told in the pictures I took, in rapid succession, of the many faces of Glenda Landry as she tried to chew and swallow this piece of ooey gooey.

What a trouper! All is well that ends well…she got us the tour!"

95 JAPAN REVISITED

In 1991, the full company went on what is called the Non-no tour, not because they had a bad time, but because that was the name of the company sponsoring the expedition. That year was a kind of Canada-Japan cultural exchange, honouring both the Charlottetown Festival and the Royal Winnipeg Ballet, starring their great ballerina, Evelyn Hart.

Max Reimer went along as CEO of what he says was his thirteenth production of our musical. He had started out on stage as Cecil the farmer and at a sold-out matinee in Charlottetown, his Mennonite mother had to sit in the pit beside Fen Watkin. Max says she never really noticed his few lines of dialogue because she kept looking for the Anne of Thea McNeil. Max eventually worked his way from farmer, to choreographer, to business manager, and to directing his own production of *"Anne of Green Gables"* at Theatre Aquarius, in Hamilton.

In Japan in 1991 he was both choreographer and company manager. He remembers being treated by the Japanese as if he was pure gold. He said: "It became embarrassing" If Max saw something he liked in a shop, before he knew it, the thing was gift wrapped and waiting for him in his hotel room. Whenever he was in a bar he never had an empty glass, as it was always refilled by his hosts.

It must have been his job as money man that engendered such respect. When it came time to pay off the company, Max was taken to a bank, but it wasn't a formal transaction. It was more like a drug deal as he was slipped an envelope in the middle of a bank and told not to count it till he got to his hotel room. The amount, three million yen in cash (about $250,000) was exactly what the Japanese told him to expect. Max had to make several trips from his hotel room to the desk downstairs to get the right amount of notes to pay the cast.

His most vivid cultural memory of the whole trip was singing "My Way" (he's a dancer, not a singer) in a Karoake bar. The Japanese applauded respectfully while the Charlottetown cast hooted with derision. Evidently in Japan you get respect whether or not you stink as a vocalist.

For more details of this tour, I am forever indebted to Denise Fergusson because of a series of articles she wrote for the St. Mary's Journal-Argus, the newspaper in the Ontario town where she now resides. I am so thankful for her zeal and kindness in responding to my request for stories of that tour.

Although she spent nine years with the Festival as Rachel Lynde, in the two tours of *"Anne of Green Gables"* in Japan, Denise played Marilla. Incidentally, on one tour, the part of Prissy Andrews was played by Justine

Campbell, a professional dancer, who had wanted to jump on stage and be part of the action ever since she was a small child accompanying her parents, Norman and Elaine.

This 1991 Japan tour had a separate cast complete with understudies from the company occupying the Festival main stage. There was a five week rehearsal period and a special Charlottetown opening for the would-be ambassadors taking

Justine Campbell as "Prissy" and other Avonlea Beauties

the show abroad. Not a trace of rivalry between the two companies. They sat in on each other rehearsals and cheered each other's opening nights. So many friendships were formed, so much laughter resounded backstage, so much talent under one roof.

Both companies were very different in personality, look and design. Wardrobe even provided different costumes from those of the home team. It was as if each cast performed a different story, with the same script, plot and characters!

The whole Charlottetown company showed up at the airport to wish their fellow travelers Bon Voyage and God speed. Many photos were taken, tears flowed and hugs and kisses were distributed all around.

Although the performances in Japan were in English, all summer long the cast, understudies and crew had been taking Japanese language lessons twice weekly, they wanted to be able to greet and meet the guests in their own language at post performances parties. They had many occasion to practice their phrasebooks and Japan tour guides books knowledge on unsuspecting Japanese tourists in Charlottetown. The tourists themselves were quite astonished and frequently delighted.

Denise "Marilla" and "Workers for the Cause" in Japan

Thirty-two excited actors, dancers plus two musicians jetted to Vancouver on Canadian Airlines flight 907, wearing their red and white *"Anne of Green Gables"* Japan tour jackets, the colours of both Japanese and Canadian flags.

After losing a day en route thanks to the International Date line, they were in Tokyo to join their director, stage management staff and crew and to meet the additional Japanese contingent of eighteen musicians, twenty four crew members and twelve interpreters who would travel with the company through all seven cities over the next eight weeks. The fact that there was a 4.7 earthquake the night they arrived was lost in the excitement of finally being there.

"Anne of Green Gables," The Musical opened in Tokyo on Canada Day at the beautiful Theatre Cocoon in the dazzling Bukamura three-theaters Complex, before a glittering audience that included members of Japan's Royal Family, various embassy officials and representatives of the Canadian Government.

According to "Marilla" Fergusson, it was quite a night. Dozens and dozens of bouquets of flowers were thrown onto the stage at curtain call followed by fourteen company curtain calls, in addition to the kudos for individual performers. Five of the principals were invited to a special tea ceremony afterwards with more flowers and more gifts. The *"Anne of Green Gables"* fan club was waiting for the performers outside by the Stage Door as they were trying to lug their newly acquired loot into a taxi.

That week there were nine performances, and at long last, a day off to rest and shake off the rest of what Denise's little Japanese dresser called 'Jet Rag.' Most of the cast opted to visit the city of Tokyo. It was hot, with temperatures in the mid thirties. Denise visited the Kabuki theater and other historical sites while some of our Canucks seemed to go mad buying up video equipment, cameras and oh yes…pearls. (in homage to Matthew's horse, I suppose). Ooooh the shopping!

Others went on to visit temples, shrines, museums, and the pandas at the Ueno zoo.

The following day was a reception given by Ambassador Taylor at the stunning new Canadian Embassy. Princess Nori of the Royal House came but no one got a chance to practice their Japanese because this tiny, shy 21 year old Princess spoke impeccable English.

148

Here is a statement by Denise Fergusson that may make you sit up and take notice. "Tokyo is one of the safest cities in the world; street crime is virtually unknown, and I can walk about freely and get deliciously lost all by myself if the mood strikes me.

Not many people speak English and very few of the streets have signs of any kind except for the major thoroughfares. The clean, efficient subway has many lines, and they are not always marked in letters we can recognize, but everyone is so helpful and with a lot of pointing and use of dictionaries and phrase books, everyone manages in seeing the city and eating up a storm. Food is delicious, plentiful and inexpensive, contrary to what we had heard, all we have to do is avoid the hotels and expense account restaurants and bars."

Remember this was 1991, before the 15 year recession that Japan experienced. Norman Campbell told me that when he and Elaine visited in 2002, a cup of coffee and toast in a first rate Tokyo hotel cost him fifty bucks!

Denise continues: "although I am very tall and very fair-haired to Japanese eyes, one never feels alien or out of place. No one stares, so you are afforded a privacy amidst the teeming masses. Even waiting on a crowded street corner, everyone leaves a few feet of space between themselves and the next person. Aside from Westerners, I haven't seen a plump person the entire time I've been here." (What! No Sumo wrestlers? I think by Westerners, Denise meant our white race. I don't think she was referring to Albertans and the Calorie Stampede.)

Denise made many friends during her visits to Japan, and she still goes back there to visit them. She says that even though it has been fifteen years since her last tour with our musical, complete strangers will smile at her on a Tokyo street and shyly say the word that identifies her for them: "Herro Marirrer!"

96 ROST IN TRANSRATION

Outside of Tokyo, very few Japanese speak English, yet there are often signs in English that purport to give information and even instructions;

"Use this erevator. Fright elevator is repair."

"Dresses for Ladies and Gentlemen"

Costumumes for Rent" (presumably costume)

"Drink Coca Cola and Splite." (Sprite)

Marilla came out in Japanese sounding like Madira!"

Lorraine Foreman, playing Mrs. Lynde', (Missa Rind) gave the Japanese dressers a lot of pronunciation problems. They settled for Rolo for Lorraine.

Attempts to speak Japanese sometimes caused problems too. In one instance, Christina Gordon asked an astonished Japanese waitress "where the washroom was" what she actually said was "Am I a toilet?" " Everyone is so patient while we struggle. There was no end to politeness and friendliness shown to our entire cast and crew while in Japan."

97 ANOTHER KIND OF KYOTO ACCORD

Denise and the rest of our traveling ambassadors from Charlottetown moved from Tokyo to the Kaiken Theatre in Kyoto,

Denise wrote in her column: There are 1600 temples (Buddhist) and 270 shrines (Shinto) a sightseer's paradise, enfolded by scenic hills, canals, dotted with gardens and stores, and crowned (to me) by a most impressive sight The dazzling Golden Pavilion of the Kinkakuji Temple mirrored in a smooth reflecting pond. The Taj Mahal could hardly equal this.

We rounded a corner of the pathway right after a sudden downpour with soft thunder rumbling in the distance. The leaves were shimmering as the raindrops slowly dripped off them, and the smells of earth and moss and camellias were almost overpowering. And there it was, across the pond, a golden glow of a structure, almost dreamlike as so much of ancient Japan appears to our North American eyes. Everyone gasped. That moment is one that will remain high on the memory bank of all who were there."

Kyoto is also the home of the Noh Theater, with a rich cultural and artistic history.

(As in the song: "There's no Theatre like Noh Theater." Sorry about that Denise, please continue.)

High into the Kyoto Hills in the shade of Kodaiji Temple I sat between 'Rain Shower House' and 'Umbrella House', tea-houses designed by a 16th century tea-master, continually bumping into both Canadian and Japanese cast and crew members. "We can't escape each other."

After much photography I climbed further up the mountain past Koyasu-Hoto (Easy Child Birth Pavilion), to a garden of such tranquillity, before realizing it was past 4:15, and what a rush to get down to where taxis could be found to get back to the hotel, then on to Kyoto Kaikich Hall for the 6:30 curtain. All this in a hundred and one degrees temperature!

Aside from doing the show itself, and rubbernecking visits to temples, the cast and crew devoted themselves to shopping expeditions. They made their pilgrimage to the Handicraft Center. Japanese dolls, kimonos and T-shirts being displayed from room to room. It has become Green Gables shopping Tour from Canada. What drew our bunch to the cash registers? The place was Pentax heaven.

Kyoto is probably the most photographed city in all of Japan, and for good reasons. Every corner or alley-way is a photo-op. Especially the Gion district where the geishas, so delicate and doll-like in kimonos and wooden clogs, can be seen scurrying along preparing for the evening's entertainment.

Denise never stopped touristing. She bought a hundred yen fortune that was translated for her by two young girls, both great fans of Anne (everyone in Kyoto is, apparently.) The fortune predicted good luck (Surprise! Surprise!) and if tied to the tree at the Shrine it would further that predicted good luck and cancel anything negative on the forecast. For Denise it was all good fun and worth the 80 cents Canadian to meet so many people willing to translate.

"The fine thing about Kyoto is the accessibility of the bus system, every-where else we are buried in the subways tunnels as bus routes are too slow and incomprehensible. No English is spoken, yet somehow the locals do their best to communicate and everybody seems to get by."

The company played double shows on most of their days, noon and 4:15. Opening week in Tokyo they did 8 shows in 5 days, plus the opening night party and the closing night party. In Kyoto, right after the Thursday double show the cast rushed off to the Tenjin Matsuri shrine to see great blazing floats on the river, and share food with people in kimonos carrying lanterns.

The next day is a day off and it's on to Nara, the ancient capital, to visit the giant Buddha at Todaiji Temple. This great bronze Buddha was built 1200 years ago by Emperor Shomu. Despite the 101 degree heat some of the cast walked around Nara for six and a half hours. They fed the deer on the grounds of the Temple with the buckwheat cakes that are on sale every-where. The deer bow their heads to us, like Japanese people bow to each other before they eat, then after, as thanks. We are astonished. Deer are con-sidered heavenly messengers, and return to their pens at the sound of the temple trumpet at dusk. A long time ago an early ruler was reported to have come to Nara on the back of a white-tailed deer and he prospered, and the deer have been held in reverence ever since.

Denise goes on: "I'd like to tell you where we all went after that, but I ran out of buckwheat cakes, and a deer ate most of my carefully marked map."

Sunday a visit to Mount Fuji in a deep fog.(I know its out there somewhere!) The tour is now referred to as "Marilla in the mist." A volcanic hot springs is visible down the mountain, and to eat eggs boiled in their sulfurous waters gives, we are told, Long Life, (and also considerable indigestion.)

Then it's onto the bullet train to Osaka

Cast and crew are lodged in a truly Japanese hotel which is also a spa, at a place called Atami. Futons on the floor, no furniture, but (thank God) a Western toilet, not the dreaded hole in the floor and hold-on-for-dear-life to that rope which was often encountered. Also a Flower bath for the gals, a Roman bath for the guys followed by hot sake and relaxing in incredible computerized massage chairs. Everyone sleeps like logs despite the hard futons and millet pillows. Some brave a Japanese breakfast, wondering what the hell it was that they ate, but it stays down.

Then downtown Atami, which is full of young people in Happy Coats and headbands carrying portable shrines. More dancing and chanting, and the Anne bunch join in along with a bunch of Aussies. Lots of laughter and picture-taking and Commonwealth bonding. All this in the blazing heat…upper thirties. Fortunately there are fruit juice machines everywhere. All kinds of juices and green tea at from seventy to one hundred yen a shot, that's sixty to eighty five cents. Coffee costs the same in a machine, but coffee in the hotel is as much as a complete meal, five bucks. Beer in a dispensing machine is even cheaper than a soft drink!

Thirsts quenched, everybody piles on the bullet train to Nagoya, a city that was flattened by saturation bombing during the war, and totally rebuilt by the Americans to look like Washington D.C. (minus the crime.) Highlights are a visit to Tokugwa Museum, and a traveling exhibit of European art of Monet, Picasso and Modigliani paintings.

Then on the 220 km. an hour bullet train to Osaka, home of the 1970 World's Fair where our musical Anne first showed herself to this grateful nation.

Osakas is a gleaming city completely rebuilt for commerce, (this time the Japanese did it right.) "I try not to think of the bombings and that my new friends were once such dreaded enemies. Next stop is Hiroshima. It won't be easy going to that memorial."

Welcome to Expo 70 Gracie Finley, Jeff Hyslop and Island Groupies

In Osaka the cast stays at the Grand Hotel, which contains the 2600 seat Festival Hall with its seventy-three feet wide stage. Certain musical numbers like the picnic races and the buggy ride have to be adjusted to this extra space. Denise says: "My dressing room is as large as my living room at home in St. Mary's. It's complete with sofas, sliding panels, private bath and shower."

And always in attendance at every show, the loyal *"Anne of Green Gables"* fan club. Fans and autograph seekers deluge the cast with gifts as they come out the stage door. After the show, the cast rents boats on the river with candles in paper lanterns. Christine Gordon and Denise had the task of convincing the rental man that females can handle a rowboat. He was skeptical. Our Japanese interpreter is skeptical too (she's a great help!) "But we do better than the guys, skimming back into dock after great fun bobbing about the river with other cast members. The rental man is impressed. He gives out pins, then we watch the fireworks and share laughter with total strangers who don't speak English and it really doesn't matter."

"We're doing fine, the show is a joy to play and there is so much to see and do. Another leave-taking ahead. (Sigh) So many moments to cherish. I wanted to go back to the Oriental Museum of Ceramics but tomorrow is our last day here, so with a day off, we wanted to board the train out of town to (they claim) Japan's finest castle. …if the typhoon doesn't hit us! Otherwise we'll just stay here on our day off and eat. There is a saying that Osaka people eat out until they go bankrupt. Inexpensive restaurants are everywhere. Ate an omelet the other day… they gave me a fork! It seemed so unwieldy and heavy, we're not used to them anymore."

After Osaka came Hiroshima. Denise said it was a deeply moving and profound experience for everyone. The theater where they performed was close to the epicenter where the A-bomb was dropped on August 8th, 1945. The people of Hiroshima have turned their horror into a positive place for all of mankind. They proudly proclaim "No more Hiroshimas" when they display the building called the A-bomb Dome, which has been left in its skeletal state to keep as reminder of the devastation. "Children playing close to the gutted remains brought tears to the eyes." She visited the Peace Museum, only half a block from the theater, and the surrounding park with beautiful origami and flowers at the base of every one of the monuments.

Only three performances in Hiroshima but many bouquets on stage which were so large the cast could hardly hold them. Then on to a well deserved break on the island of Kyushu, with palm fronds playing in tropical breezes. The Anne Academy's legion of fans take the cast sight-seeing to Fukuoka Castle, and along with 500,000 people they watch the best fireworks display our actors are ever likely to see.

Max Reimer, the company manager and choreographer was in that dense crowd with his young son, when he noticed a little Japanese boy disappear momentarily after being accidentally stepped on in the crush. Max and others of the Anne company spent their time scooping up Japanese children and returning them to their parents.

Denise says she didn't see any other gaijins there (foreigners like herself).

A great night for Canada-Japanese relations.

Hank Stinson and his wife Rowena, have their own story to tell and I'll let him tell it: "We were welcomed with open arms everywhere we went in

Japan, but most of all in a little town near Fukuoka where they teach English in a school called "The Anne Academy." The warmth and generosity of Kiomi Matsufugi and her colleagues was truly impressive and the bonds of friendship formed there will last a lifetime." Recently Rowena's school principal, Nellie Aitken, was diagnosed with terminal cancer. Rowena mentioned this in a letter to Kiomi and, shortly afterward received a parcel containing one thousand paper cranes made by our friends at the Anne Academy. These cranes, along with a thousand more made by the staff and friends of Nellie Aitken, may be seen hanging from the ceilings the entire length of the corridor at the Westwood Primary School in Cornwall, P.E.I. Hank says Nellie is doing very well.

Back to their favorite city, Kyoto, the company plays the only small center of the tour, in nearby Ohmihatchiman on Lake Biwa. (small place, big name). Denise says it was relaxing to play in a smaller theater after that seventy three foot stage in Osaka.

Hank Stinson said a horrific incident happened during the store scene where Matthew tries to buy the dress with puffed sleeves. Hank, as the stationmaster, was onstage with the actors playing Cecil the farmer (220 pounds) and Earl the mailman. (130 pounds). Among the many objects passed around beginning with the letter "P" was a large jar of pickles. The actor playing the farmer must have been day-dreaming, because he was late by four beats into the song that Lucilla sings to Matthew. Realizing he was late to pass the pickle jar to the Mailman, he threw it across the stage to the mailman anyway, who also must have been daydreaming because it caught him on the side of the head. He had blood gushing down the side of his head and frantically whispered to Hank: "I think I'm hit! What should I do?" Hank said: "Get off the stage, you're bleeding all over the counter!" Twenty four hours later he was back on stage. The audience may not have been in stitches, but Earl the mailman certainly was.

Next stop was Yokohama. More bullet train, more adulation from Japanese audiences, especially the little groupies lining up at the stage door for both Leisa Way as Anne and Doug Adler as Gilbert. Leisa was big stuff on the teeny-bopper circuit and Doug was a big hottie, because he had already done a solo concert in Japan the year before, all arranged by a female fan.

On to Tokyo and the trip home, so many memories and so many new friends.

98 WISH FULFILLMENT

There is a cookbook compiled by many cast members of our musical. Denise Fergusson says it came out of the bake sales that were held backstage at matinees and sold to the cast, crew and musicians. Proceeds went to various Charlottetown charities,

One of the cast's favorites charity was The Children's Wish Foundation, because the kids whose wishes were realized would come to see the show and then visit backstage.

One of them was a little girl from Australia, Kassandra Hall, a nine year old with a rare form of stomach cancer, and given the precarious state of her health, had her wish of seeing Anne of Green Gables in PEI granted.

Bake sale, Denise Ferguson and Liz Mawson. "Tarts for Sale"

In May 1991, four months after she had completed chemotherapy she had her wish granted by The Children's Wish Foundation. She came to Charlottetown all the way from Down Under with her mom and dad and sister Lyndell. Lee Gauthier, from the Children's Wish, arranged for them to visit the Anne house in Cavendish, escorted by the PEI head of Parks Canada, and the park was closed to the public while they were there. Kassie has remained friends with Lee and his extended family and in the summer of 2007, she came back to PEI with her mom to attend a family wedding.

When they arrived in May of '91 the show was not on, but fortunately it was at the time the two companies were rehearsing, one for the Festival season, the other for a Japan tour and they were invited to watch the rehearsals.

This was particularly exciting for Kassie as she had started singing and dancing on stage at three years old, and held dreams of future stardom. The plan was for the sisters to visit for one hour but ended up staying the whole day and mom and dad had a few precious hours alone in Charlottetown. By the end of the day Kassie knew the songs by heart (and still does) and made some life long friends. Kassie amazed everyone with her stamina and energy, they were taken to lunch by the cast, and later visited Denise Fergusson's cottage at Rice Point.

She went home with a poster and a doll, and was so ecstatic that it seemed to give her the courage to go on with further therapies. Her particular thrill was having a lot of attention lavished on her by Anne herself, Leisa Way, who was in Charlottetown for five seasons from 1987-91 the tour in Japan and returned for the season of 1993.

I'll let Leisa tell you more about Kassie.

"The first night that Kassie came to the show (actually it was a full-dress rehearsal) the whole cast met her after the show and we had a party for her. She was a beautiful child, even with no hair. Talk about a face lighting up with pleasure, I will never forget how happy she was during that visit. She made an impression on all of us for her courage in the face of the unthinkable. Kassie remained in contact with some of the cast through e-mails. Despite the fact that it was necessary to remove one of her kidneys because of a different kind of cancer attack, Kassie is now a young woman in her late twenties and she's been back to the Island not once, but twice, last time…the summer of 2007."

In December 2007 Leisa Way tells me she has just heard from Kassie who is about to turn 30. She has battled cancer eight different times. Leisa thinks that with her record of dauntless courage Kassandra is bound to prevail. She is still living in Australia, was married a few years ago, and is resigned to the fact that because of her treatments she will never have children. She and her hubby Michael are the proud parents of 2 dogs named Elvis and Sunny."

She goes on "I always have enjoyed seeing the pictures she has sent me, and I feel blessed to know this very special girl. It was a hard letter to read this time because Kass is sick yet again. But her letter was so hopeful and positive. Even after *"KASSIE HALL"*

157

all these years, every time we talk or write, she continues to be one of the most positive people I have ever met. I suppose that is why she has been able to beat this cancer so many times. I pray that she is able to fight this fight again. I pray that next year, and for years to come, I will continue to be blessed with her friendship. Her friendship is yet another gift that Anne has given to me."

I got an email from Kassie this January. She does indeed sound like a very special young woman. This is an excerpt of what she wrote to Claudette and I.

"PEI and "ANNE" remains so special to me, it changed my life and despite the reasons that took me to PEI initially, I wouldn't change a moment of it, for the enduring friendships I have made are just so important to me. Who could possibly have known that a book written 100 years ago could impact so many lives—my own, that of my family and these wonderful, generous people who took us into their hearts and homes. PEI is now my "other home" and I would live there in a flash if only I could. As for the freckle-faced red-head, she will always be my friend and someone who brought more happiness to me that she could ever know."

99 ANNE OF DISABLED

I have been asked many times what was the most moving performance of our musical that I have ever seen. I don't need to hesitate or think about it. It was a performance put on by the kids of the Hugh Macmillan Center, formerly called the Ontario Crippled Children Center. Politically incorrect? That's nothing. During the forties I remember going past their headquarters on Bloor Street, near what is now the Mount Pleasant extension, where there was a huge sign over the door that blared out "THE HOME FOR INCURABLES." Now the facility is known as Bloorview Children's Hospital.

The main reason we wanted to do this very special version of our musical was to enable the disabled to show how able they were.

My involvement with all this began with an Easter Seals telethon in Parry Sound in 1974. I was on board as Charlie Farquharson, a fake Parry Hooter (that's what they call themselves). The special guest was Whipper Watson, born Billy Potts, a retired wrestler and former World champion, who had made this charity his own particular quest. In the middle of the telethon, Whipper suddenly challenged me to an arm wrestling contest. The astounding thing is that I won. This was true charity on his part. I told Whipper that any outfit that was as corrupt as his were my kind of people.

So I spent the next 25 years as his court jester, trailing around after him on the banquet circuit where Whipper made his serious speech about helping disabled kids. Together we raised money for projects to enable the disabled, who face more challenges, hurdles and obstacles in a day than most of us do during our entire lives.

Thinking of zipping downtown Toronto by bus or subway? Be grateful you don't have a wheelchair along. But then you say...surely there is something called Wheel-Trans? One of the former Timmys, Spencer Miller, refers to the service as Feel-Trans: "they pick you up when they bloody well feel like it!"

For example, Torontonians take the subway as a means of transportation. But there are only six subway stops on the entire Metropolitan Toronto network that are wheelchair accessible. New buses do a better job, one thousand out of fifteen hundred and sixty buses have either a lift or a ramp or a kneeling feature (whatever that is, milord), and have two wheelchair/scooter positions on a fully accessible bus and some optional tie-downs. Never heard of all this? A blue light beside the destination sign or the international wheelchair symbol indicates that the bus is indeed wheelchair accessible. The lift ramps can also accommodate older citizens who use walkers, crutches, canes and scooters.

Reggie Topping "Easter Seals' Timmy," Don Harron

Trevor Black

Fen Watkin, Malcolm Black,
Don Harron, Michelle Kungel,
Andrea Pachenko

Through the years working with Whipper Watson I got to know several of these so-called disabled kids. Each year a Timmy and a Tammy is nominated from among their number to carry the torch for Easter Seals. Often these kids were riding on Whipper's shoulder at sports banquets till it got to be considered politically incorrect.

The person who was really in charge of the Timmys and Tammys was Susan Brower, a volunteer worker who knew Whip well because she had been married to another wrestler, Bulldog Brower. Consequently there were always pro-wrestlers about to help in any charity drives for the disabled. Sue Brower herself could have been mistaken for a lady wrestler. She had a heart as big as her frame, and with her, the kids always came first, not the organization or her job within it.

It was Sue Brower, not me, who first got the idea that her kids should do their own presentation of our Anne musical. I was happy to climb aboard but when she asked me to direct the production, I remembered my former one-time experience with Louis Riel, decided against it and called in a professional.

Malcolm Black has directed thirty three musicals on the professional stage in the United States and Canada. I had known him both in Hollywood and at the Stratford Connecticut Shakespeare Festival. Malcolm accepted this freebie without hesitation.

I also asked Fen Watkin, longtime musical director of the Charlottetown Festival to give us some help with the intricacies of the musical score. Fen came to the first rehearsal and gave advice to John Hughes, our musical director, who was invaluable throughout the remainder of the rehearsals and the shows themselves.

Casting was done without any kids having to audition for the part. We knew what we were looking for.

Anne was a fifteen year old minx called Andrea Pachenko. Her physical disability was that her two arms stopped at the elbow, but it didn't impede her vivaciousness one bit. She became a vibrantly saucy Anne.

Marilla was a fourteen year old in a wheel-chair, Laura Booth, but unconfined in her calm intelligence which looked a lot like maturity.

Matthew was one of the former Timmys, Reggie Topping (and the last one ever to sit on Whipper's shoulder), a twenty year old with spina bifida, on crutches, who was already an experienced amateur actor. Reggie is becoming an inter-

Reggie Topping, Don Harron, John Hughes, Davina Manhas

esting writer currently working on a whodunit with a disabled detective solving crimes.

Mrs. Rachel Lynde, the big-mouthed town gossip, was definitely cast against type. The role was taken by a nine-year-old diminutive East Asian girl, Davina Manhas, who had to use a walker to propel her tiny body forward.

Anne's nemesis, Josie Pye, was more of a type-cast; Michelle Kungle loved rap and hip hop, but agreed to participate in our more staid musical efforts.

The heart-throb role of Gilbert Blythe was given to a wisp of a boy called Adam Barber, not terribly interested in theater, but more of a serious jock in a wheelchair who would rather be playing floor hockey or basketball. He went along with our project with a shy non-show bizzy indifference, and during our rehearsals at the Bloorview auditorium he could often be found next door in the gym, watching group sports.

The role of Tillie Boulter, one of Anne's school chums, is a minor one in terms of dialogue, only a couple of lines. Danny Harder was cast as Tillie, she was one of the Bloorview residents designated as non-verbal; she was unable to speak but was definitely very vocal. She spent all her time lying on a hospital gurney and she communicated through her fingers, tapping out messages in the form of Bliss symbols on a computer board in front of her. Danny became a vital part of the presentation. The other actors would read out to the audience what she had written, and Danny would roar with delight. The night of the show itself which opened with civic officials making speeches about the occasion, their words were interrupted by Danny's roars of impatience in the wings for the "old folks" to get off the stage and let the real purpose of the evening commence. Eventually they did. At other unexpected times during the performance she would squeal her delight at being part of the company. If anybody was the true spirit of unbridled joy in overcoming an overwhelming disability it was our Danny. Her mother, Karen, told me that this particular experience was a new beginning for her daughter, because after our show finished (and we did it more than once) Danny went on to do a lot of things she had previously shirked.

Spencer Miller, previously mentioned as a vocal wheelchair opponent of Wheel-Trans, was chosen as the teacher Mr. Phillips. Spencer is now a motivational speaker addressing school children, athletic teams and business organizations, giving encouragement to the disadvantaged (and believe me, disadvantaged businessmen are going to need lots of encouragement in the future as I see it.)

Very early in rehearsals Malcolm found that he required surgery for prostate cancer. He got his friend Desmond Ellis to take over the last couple of rehearsals and the actual "get-in" to the theater, it made for a seamless transition. Malcolm won't soon forget that when he was forced to leave the company, Spencer followed after him into the parking lot to tell him: "Don't worry, Malcolm, I've had lots of operations and it's never as bad as you think it is going to be."

We decided that the part of Miss Stacy, the new teacher should be played by a professional singer. We were lucky enough to get the services of Priscilla Wright, who had made the top of the Canadian hit parade with her hit single recording of "Man in a Raincoat." She bonded immediately with the kids and made a suggestion to add a song that our kids could really do justice to, "We Rise Again!"

Anne's best friend Diana Barry was played by a feisty little girl, Amanda Herman, who took no nonsense from anybody, and led the cast in the rousing finale "Ice Cream." I say finale because that's where our version of the show ended. It was thought it would be enough due to their physical limitation. For obvious reasons there were no dance numbers, and the acting of the script required enormous amounts of energy. How wrong I was. After the first performance, the kids wanted to do it again, with most of the second Act included.

First, we had to get through the first opening night at Toronto's newest big theater, the Ford Center for the Performing Arts, which had already exhibited a revival of Showboat, a touring production of Sunset Boulevard, and a brand new musical, Ragtime, before it went on to Broadway. But that was not the venue chosen for our musical. We performed in the Ford Center Music Hall, possessor of the finest acoustics in any Toronto theater.

Anne was only part of a full evening entertainment. It began with speeches from various civic officials, including the Lieutenant Governor Hal Jackman. He was followed by Mayor Mel Lastman explaining the difference between his title Your Worship and the method of addressing Hal's office as Your Honour. That's why, Mel said, you honour your lieutenant governor but you worship your mayor.

The opening of the Bloorview show was the most spectacular entrance for *Anne* you could imagine. It happened one day at rehearsal that one of the kids tied his wheelchair to another one, and before the rehearsal ended they formed a chain of wheelchairs. When a railroad whistle was given to the kid in the front wheelchair, Anne was piggy backed onto the last one, you had Anne arriving as she does in the novel…by rail.

That night, since we only did the first act of our musical, it was felt that the evening should be filled out with something else besides political speeches. Wayne and Shuster had just done a spoof of Anne on their television show called Sam of Green Gables. I decided to do a Yiddish version called "Anne of Green Bagels."

Don Harron, Marilyn & Mel Lastman, Malcolm Black

Trevor Black

When I was churning out my Green Bagels version, I had envisaged Mel Lastman and his vivacious wife Marilyn to play the parts of Matthew and Marillele (Yiddish for Marilla). I took them to lunch and found that they were both too shy to be actors. Who would have believed that? (Answer: Noooooooobody!!)

A couple of years later, I did get Mel to perform one line at a benefit for the Stratford Festival when Ed Mirvish provided us with the Royal Alex. The show was called "The Shaming of the True," directed by Malcolm Black, featuring newly-elected Premier of Ontario Bob Rae as musical director who composed a melody for my lyrics "Under the NDP" (now lost in oblivion). Bob also played the leading role of Hamlet, and the leader of the Opposition, Mike Harris, Mark Anthony. Mike offered Malcolm Black the opportunity of rehearsing him privately in his office.

Hal Jackman, our Lieutenant Governor, a leading actor in his college days, cast himself as a humble peasant begging Bob Rae on bended knee to grant him a new opera house. Hal asked me to let him wear Charlie Farquharson's tattered sweater for the occasion. As for Mel Lastman, dressed in an Elizabethan costume with orange striped tights, he pushed a rack of dresses labeled Honest Ed's across the stage, stopped in the middle and said to the audience: "The quality of Mirvish is not strained!"

Turned down by the shy Lastman for the part of Matthew, I managed to get the services of Royalty, the King of Kensington himself, Al Waxman. As Marillelle, we luckily got Sylvia Lennick. I recently talked to her on the phone and learned that she is ninety-two years young! Sylvia will be forever immortalized as Caesar's wife in the Wayne and Shuster version of the Roman classic scene, where she shouts throughout the sketch: "Don't Go, Julie Don't go!" Speaking of Julie, the part of the little shicksha Anne (that's a female goy) was played by Sylvia's daughter of that name (Julie, not Anne). Malcolm Black staged it. My script went okay, but it couldn't top what those kids in their walkers and wheelchairs did to the audience in that hall.

The people connected with the Bloorview Children's Hospital who couldn't get to see our sold-out show, requested that we perform the play again in their facility. It was a gymnasium with a proscenium stage attached. This time our kids performed in front of an audience of only two hundred people. But there was no lack of enthusiasm, especially among the cast who added an abridged version of Act Two.

Priscilla Wright couldn't make it as Miss Stacy so her place was taken by Alison Giddens, who I seem to remember was on staff. The kids did a rousing version of "If It Hadn't Been For Me" and "We Rise Again."

We did that longer version of Anne a couple of months later at WindReach Farm, near Whitby. This farm is owned by Sandy Mitchell, a great philanthropist who provides horses to ride for disabled people of all ages. They ride around an Olympic size dressage ring, which is open to them all year round. A disabled child on a beautiful horse looks like an Emperor. Sandy Mitchell knows this better than any of us because he has cerebral palsy but he competes in Equestrian events and won a Medal in the Special Olympics held in Greece.

The venue at WindReach was on the main floor of the barn. It was even more intimate than the Bloorview gymnasium, because the main floor of the barn holds far fewer than two hundred people. But that's not counting the animal population in the barn beneath us, our dialogue was sometimes overwhelmed by the deafening bleating of sheep, llamas, and even horses in the pens below our stage.

A Critic with Don Harron

One final note. When I use the term "we" about the show at Wind Reach I have to confess that the actress who played Josie Pye couldn't make it to the barn at the last minute, so book in hand, I had to fill in the best I could for her. A little girl in the front row, obviously a critic, booed my performance.

A couple of years ago I did a benefit called "Home Sweet Homeless" at the Princess of Wales Theater. It was the last presentation on that stage before they opened "The Lord of the Rings." (I never did go to see that show. I figured it was just Conrad Black cleaning out his own bathtub.)

For that occasion, I wrote an opening sketch about Mother Goose being thrown out on the street with all her nursery rhyme brood. It was called "Mother Goosed!"and I called upon two Bloorview grads to help me out. I cast Spencer Miller as Simple Simon, and Reggie Topping as Peter Pumpkin Eater. We added three members from our "*Anne*" in Charlottetown: Heidi Ford as Little Bo Peep, Jennifer Toulmin as Little Red Riding Hood and Sean Hauk as Little boy Blue. Also part of the cast were Luba Goy as Goldilocks, Mary Traynor as Miss Muffet, Raven Dauda as Mary Contrary, Joyce Gordon and Claudette as the gay couple Jacqueline and Jill. Paul Brown directed and Chris Humphreys did a super job of providing the rehearsal place for us at St George the Martyr Church. Other volunteer performers were comedians Ron James, Colin Mochrie and Patrick McKenna, singers Michael Burgess and Jay Douglas, and a trio of outrageously funny drag-queens called The B-Girls. Our orchestra was under the direction of David Warrack. This show had as Mistress of Ceremonies the elegant and witty Erin Davis of radio station CHFI. It all came together thanks to brilliant Annie Allan, Charlottetown Festival's artistic director.

Spencer remembers the introduction to our Mother Goosed sketch by Erin Davis, how she talked about himself and Reggie as if they were just like the rest of the cast.

Too soon after the production of Anne at WindReach Farm we lost Danny Harder, our Bliss symbolist with the captivating roar. A lot of us from that Anne cast turned up at her funeral, and many tears flowed. Sad to say I was out of the country when the kids patron saint, Sue Brower died of cancer. Those young people who brought me that most special *Anne of Green Gables"* will never forget both Susan Brower and Danny Harder.

100 ANNE OF SASKATCHEWAN

Samuel French has looked after stock and amateur productions of our musical for many years. Every month they get on an average about two and a half pages of requests from schools, camps, and regional theaters for stock or amateur productions.Recently I got a hand-written request from Kathy Thiessen, a woman who runs a theater in the little town of Rosthern, Saskatchewan, situated between Saskatoon and Prince Albert. It has a population of about fifteen hundred but despite the paucity of population, there has been many years of live theater in a building that used to be a train station. It has been turned into an art gallery and a theater for 140 people by this amazing Thiessen woman.

Last summer for example she did a complete summer season with Michael Healey's play that has become a Canadian classic "The Drawer

Rosthern, Saskatchewan, the set for Act One, Scene Two.

Boy." This coming summer of 2008 she wants to celebrate the centennial of Lucy Maud's novel by mounting a production of our musical. Here's the catch; she wants to do it with a cast of six people. Not twenty-six, but six.

Kathy even suggested director Stephen Heatley for this foolhardy project. The same one who did the Healey play for her last summer. Now, this is a person I met three summers ago in P.E.I. when he was teaching in a summer drama school founded by former Charlottetown artistic director, Duncan Mcintosh. Steven lives in Vancouver and since I had planned to be there in a couple of weeks, I told the Thiessen woman to hold on to her schedule until Steven and I had conferred.

On a three days train trip to from Toronto to Vancouver, I started to plot out this impossible dream. I figured it might be possible with…certainly not six…but possibly seven actors. Forget about the ladies at the church, the races at the picnic, or the rest of the kids at school. All the actors would have to play duplicate or even triplicate parts except for Anne of course. She had to be herself all through the show.

Think I'm certifiable? Maybe so. Here's the run-down for a 7 actor *Anne of Green Gables," the Musical.* Matthew has to double as the teacher, Mr. Philips. Marilla has to disguise herself (with a big blonde wig) as Prissy Andrews. This means that the bachelor brother and his spinster sister will be necking in the back row of the schoolroom, while Gilbert, Anne and Diana represent the entire student body.

The actor playing Gilbert Blythe is also the station-master and the mailman. Since there is no room for a farmer he may have to address the audience in a soliloquy: "Isn't that a caution! Mainland's bin cut off agin!" Wait! You ain't heard nothing! The actress playing Rachel Lynde has to triple herself. She has to play Anne's new bosom friend, Diana, as well as the new teacher Miss Stacy. (Diana will be absent from school on that particular day)

By the way there will be no church ladies at the top of the show. Rachel Lynde will be there to ask Matthew where he's going. Playing the part of Josie Pye in this production you will double as Mrs. Barry, triple as Mrs. Blewett, and quadruple as Lucilla, the flirt in Blair's store. No three-legged or egg-and-spoon races, but there will be ice cream. Forget about the school concert. Just an announcement by Miss Stacy about the scholarship, handed to her by the mailman (Gilbert!) and the song "If It Hadn't Been For Me" will be sung and danced by whoever is left.

Still think that Steven Heatley, Kathy Thiessen and I are stark staring out-of-our skulls? Probably. But I'm going to be there in Rosthern, Saskatchewan in that 140 seat theater on opening night July 5th. 2008.

101 FOREVER ANNE?

One of the things Norman and Elaine Campbell and I wanted most for our musical was that some day it would be a feature film. Norman had always wanted to direct it, but when the chance came to do it, he asked our old friend, the other Norman (Jewison) to do it instead. Norman J. told us he had already done two film musicals, "Fiddler on the Roof" shot in Yugoslavia, and "Jesus Christ Superstar" filmed in Israel. With a weary look on his face just remembering what he went through, Norman J. felt that those two experiences would do him for all time, thank you.

The reason the film project came up in the first place is that we had interest from a Japanese company after the box office success of the Shiki Theater productions. These Japanese gentlemen were willing to come all the way to Toronto to talk to us about it. In the meantime I set about writing a screenplay with everything that I ever wanted to include from Lucy Maud's novel. I typed 170 pages of script at the same time that I was appearing in a Toronto theater in Bernard Slade's Broadway hit "Same Time Next Year."

The Japanese arrived soon after that, not just one or two, but a delegation of four, maybe five I'm trying to remember. There were many meetings with a great deal of mutual bowing and lots of green tea. Many things were discussed, locations, staffing, billeting, but the length of the film was only revealed at the last meeting. The Japanese wanted this overlong script to take no more than a hundred minutes!

I looked at Norman. He didn't look at me. Before I could say a word he rose to his feet and he told the Japanese in no uncertain Canadian terms that they had wasted both his valuable time and theirs. I can only tell you that the fury in his usually mild-mannered voice was the second Norman Campbell tsunami I witnessed. No bows, no green tea, just a hasty exit.

That was back in 1986. Norman and Elaine are no longer with me, but I still have my copy of that script. Norman Jewison agrees with the Japanese…almost. He says in this day and age when comic books rather than novels rule the roost, the script should be no more than one hundred and ten pages.

Not long ago interest came from China. Wade McLoughlin is the head of the University of Prince Edward Island,(an institution that has given all three of us, Norman, Elaine and I, honorary degrees) and he has visited China more than once. On a recent visit he met one of those Communist billionaires who have made fortunes in real estate. Wade told me his name, but I don't think I remember it correctly. Shanghai Lil? It sounded like the name of a bar girl.

Whatever his name is, Wade talked him into visiting P.E.I. The Commie tycoon was astonished to find a place with lots of clean air and water and arable land. He said he might like to buy three or four farms on the Island, and he wondered if twenty million dollars would do it. Wade's pal, Duncan Macintosh (former Moody Spurgeon Macpherson, not to mention former artistic director of the Charlottetown Festival) said wryly to me that for twenty million dollars he could probably buy all of Prince Edward County.

I don't know what happened to the real estate deal, but I do know that Duncan interested the Red rich man in another project. He was told about the long history of our musical, how it had attracted millions of people, including many thousands from Japan. But it was the story of Anne itself that interested this government-sponsored multi-million dollar real estate investor. For the last few years the Chinese global economy has been growing by leaps and bounds to the advantage of its urban citizens, but to the detriment of its rural population.

Perhaps Mr. Oriental Moneybags had heard about the novel itself finally being published in Beijing and selling fifty thousand copies the first day. At any rate the billionaire went back to China and sent his representative to Toronto to have breakfast with Elaine, myself and Duncan Macintosh. His name was Howard Ling, and it wasn't too long a journey for him because he had an office in a distant land called Mississauga.

The breakfast went very well, partly because of Elaine's cooking, and partly because Howard talked about doing the film in English. The director was to be by one of China's great new film-makers like Ang Lee, or Yang Zimou or somebody called Shien Kaige (pronounced Cagey). We were told they all wanted to do a film about simple country people living an idyllic life with enduring values. We were well aware of Mr. Lee and his Oscar for "Humpback…(sorry) Brokeback Mountain," and also his sterling work with Jane Austen. Mr. Zimou, if I have his name correctly, was involved in dazzling films like "Raise the Red Lantern " "Hero" and "The House of Flying Daggers." Mr. Cagey had just finished an historical film about China with the biggest budget of any film so far. It all looked very exciting, and our Anne seemed to fit their desire to depict rural people on film as something noble.

Scripts and tapes were sent to Beijing. Elaine and I were invited to travel there, all expenses paid that spring for talks with whichever director would be involved. Then…silence. Howard Ling's phone in Mississauga rang and rang.

Actually he was back in China but neglected to give us his Beijing number. This was after my manager Paul Simmons had taken Howard and his charming wife to dinner and exchanged presents three times. Duncan McIntosh eventually tracked him down. The results were disappointing. Oscar winner Ang Lee was naturally up to here with film assignments for the next few years.

As for Wang Zem In…no, he's the dictator in charge of all China…Yang Zimou? Whatever. He has teamed up with Steven Spielberg to bring you the 2008 Olympics. As of now the China Syndrome is closed. The rural Chinese are still being neglected at the expense of the urban population, and their government seems to have other things on their minds, like getting the lead out of our toys, perhaps. I also think from my experience that those people over there have a very subtle superiority complex regarding us Western barbarians. After all, if you know your ancient history, the Chinese were writing poems on perfumed paper while we were still eating raw meat in caves.

Never mind. I'll keep you posted. I promise you, and you too Norman and Elaine, that there will be a feature film version made of *"Anne of Green Gables," The Musical.*

Leisa Way, "All I really wanna do is direct"

Charlottetown Festival Archives

PM MEETS UP WITH ANNE

CANWEST NEWS PHOTO

Prime Minister Jean Chretien greets actress Jennifer Toulmin who plays Anne of Green Gables Thursday in Ottawa at the touring production of the musical. The production is playing at an Ottawa theatre. See story, C3.

Ottawa newspaper

Matthew, *"I'll let Marilla Do It"*

ACTORS THROUGH THE YEARS

ANNE
Jamie Ray
Gracie Finley
Malorie-Anne Spiller
Susan Cuthbert
Thea McNeil
Tracey Moore
Leisa Way
Glynis Ranney
Tracy Michailidis
Samantha Winstanley
Sharmaine Ryan
Chilina Kennedy
Jennifer Toulmin
Amy Wallis

MARILLA
Barbara Hamilton
Mary Savidge
Elizabeth Mawson
Susan Johnston-Collins
Valerie Boyle
Judy Marshak
Janet McEwen

MATTHEW
Peter Mews
Doug Chamberlain
George Merner
Ron Hastings
Terry Doyle
Leon Pownall
David Hughes
David Renton
Bill Hosie
Hank Stinson
David Glyn-Jones
Giulio Kukurugya
Michael Fletcher
Sandy Winsby

DIANA
Marilyn Stuart
Susan Anderson
Glenda Landry
Mary Trainor
Sara Brenner
Jayne Patterson
Liz Gilroy
Kirsten Mackenzie
Lisa Rubin
Sarah Daurie
Brenley Charkow
Heidi Ford
Natalie Daradich
Allison Smith

GILBERT
Dean Regan
Jeff Hyslop
Bill Houghton
Barrie Wood
Jim White
Larry Herbert
Andrew MacBean
Brian Hill
David Hogan
Eddie Glenn
Doug Adler
Geoffrey Whynot
John McPherson
Steve Girardi
Michael Donald
Mark Prince
Stephen Patterson
Graham Coffeng
Daniel Murphy
Jamie McKnight
Sean Hauk
Louie Rosetti

THE CHARLOTTETOWN FESTIVAL AT A GLANCE

1965
Anne of Green Gables*
Laugh with Leacock*
Wayne & Shuster
Spring Thaw

1966
Anne of Green Gables*
The Ottawa Man
Private Turvey's War*

1967
Anne of Green Gables*
Paradise Hill
Yesterday the Children were Dancing
Rose Latulippe

1968
Anne of Green Gables*
Johnny Belinda*
Beyond the Fringe
Sunshine Town*

1969
Anne of Green Gables*
Johnny Belinda*
Life Can Be Like Wow*

1970
Anne of Green Gables*
Private Turvey's War*
Jane Eyre*

1971
Anne of Green Gables*
"Mary, Queen of Scots*"
Jane Eyre*
Children's Theatre*

1972
Anne of Green Gables*
Ballade*
"Mary, Queen of Scots*"
Les Feux Follets*
Squeeze*
Children's Theatre

1973
Anne of Green Gables*
Ballade*
Joey*
Les Feux Follets*

1974
Anne of Green Gables*
Kronborg: 1582*
Johnny Belinda*

1975
Anne of Green Gables*
Kronborg: 1582*
Johnny Belinda*

1976
Anne of Green Gables*
Rowdyman*
By George!*

1977
Anne of Green Gables*
By George!*
The Legend of the Dumbells*
The Road To Charlottetown*

1978
Anne of Green Gables*
Windsor*
The Legend of the Dumbells*
Eight to the Bar*
Lies and Other Lyrics*

1979
Anne of Green Gables*
On a Summer's Night*
Les Feux Follets*
Eight to the Bar*
The Family Way*
Winnie*

1980
Anne of Green Gables*
Fauntleroy&
Les Feux Follets*
Love in the Backseat*
Happily Ever After*
Come by the Hills*
Flash in the Pan*
The Tree Bears*

1981
Anne of Green Gables*
Fauntleroy*
Aimee*
Magcap*
Corcktails fot two Hundred*
The Three Bears*

1982
Anne of Green Gables*
Skin Deep*
Singin' and Dancin' TONIGHT*
My Many Husbands*
The Winkle Pickers*

THE CHARLOTTETOWN FESTIVAL AT A GLANCE *continued*

1983	1984	1985
Anne of Green Gables &	Anne of Green Gables*	Anne of Green Gables*
Johnny Belinda*	Ye Gods!*	Swing!*
Singin' & Dancin' TONIGHT*	Singin' & Dancin' TORNIGHT*	Fauntleroy*
"Step Right Up, Ladies and"	Sleeping Arrangements*	Sleeping Arrangements*
Jelly Beans*	Little Red Riding Hood*	Hansel & Gretel*
Take Five*		

1986	1987	1988
Anne of Green Gables*	Anne of Green Gables*	Anne of Green Gables*
Swing!*	Are You Lonesome Tonight?*	Are You Lonesome Tonight*
Babies—Bless Them All!*	Babies—Bless Them All!*	Alexandra—The last Empress*
Salat Water Moon	Salt Water Moon	The Mind Bogles*
Pump Boys & Dinettes	Billy Bishops Goes To War	Happy Birthday Irving*
Chris Elliot Comedy Show	Chris elliot Comedy Show	Dear Air*
Rapunzel*	Noel Coward—A Portrait!*	Rumperstilskin*
How She Lied To Her Husband	Take Two Modern Housewives and…*	New Canadian Kid
When God Comes to Breakfast	The Venerables*	"Il be back Before Midnight"
You don't Burn The Toats		The Venerables*
The Night the Raccoons Went Beserk*		
Culture Shock*		

1989	1990	1991
Anne of Green Gables*	Anne of Green Gables*	Anne of Green Gables*
Encore!*	The Strike At Putney Church*	Broue—Brew
Not Available in Stores*	Don Messer's Jubilee	A Child's Garden of Verses*
I'll Be Back Before Midnight	Les Belles Histoires de Thadde	I am a Bear
Maud for Myself*	a Damien	Lorne Elliot Comedy
Merlin and Arthur*	After Marlene!*	
	Brendan Behan: Confession of an	
	Iris Rebel*	
	Lunch with Leacock*	
	Bogeyman Blues*	
	The Island Soirees*	

1992	1993	1994
Anne of Green Gables*	Anne of Green Gables*	Anne of Green Gables*
The Great Adventure*	The Shooting of Dan McGrew	Guy Puttin'g on the Ritzs and Dolls
A Closer Walk with Patsy Cline	A Closer Walk With Patsy Cline	Dads
Le Café Acadien	The Princess and the Handmaiden	Lovers in Bedeque
Head a Tete	La Passion de Narcisse Mondoux	Pirates
	Spirit of a Nation	Rendez-vous Acadien*
		Spirit of a Nation

1995	1996	1997
Anne of Green gables*	Anne of Green Gables*	Anne of Green Gables*
Guys and Dolls	A Closer Walk With Patsy Cline	Johnny Belinda*
A Closer Walk With Patsy Cline	Rendez-vous acadien*	"2 Pianos, 4 Hands"
"Step Right Up, Ladies"	We Will Not Forget*	18 Wheels
and Jelly Beans*	Spirit of a Nation	Barachois
Rendez-vous Acadien*		Drill Queens Comedy
We Will Not Forget*		Rik Barron Family Concert
Spirit of a Nation		Somewhere in the World*

1998	1999	2000
Anne of Green Gables*	Anne of Green Gables*	Anne of Green Gables*
Johnny Belinda*	Emily*	Emily*
Letter From Wingfield Farm	Forever Plaid	Forever Plaid
Bending the Bows	Acadilac	Barachois
Barachois	Barachois	Drill Queens Comedy
Drill Queens Comedy	Drill Queen Comedy	The Conjuror Suite
Somewhere in the World*	Somewhere in the World*	Ceilidh on the Road
		Somewhere in the World*

2001	2002	2003
Anne of Green Gables*	Anne of Green Gables*	Anne of Green Gables*
Stan Rogers' A Matter of Heart	The Legend of the Dumbells*	Dracula: A Chamber Musical
"2 Pianos, 4 Hands"	If you Could Read My Mind	Fire
Ceilidh on the Road	The Music of Gordon Lightfoot*	Eight to the Bar**
Barachois	Fire	Arianna
Celtitute	Ceilidh on the Road	The Ross Family Cpmcert Series
Somewhere in the World*	Menopositive! The Musical	Barachois
	Songs of the Island*	
	The Happy Prince	
	Barbara Budd Concert Series	
	Barachois	
	Celtitute	
	Late Night at the Mack Series*	

2004	2005	2006
Anne of Green Gables*	Anne of Green Gables*	Anne of Green Gables*
Something Wonderful*	Canada Rocks! The Hits	Canada Rocks! The Hits
A Closer Walk with Patsy Cline	Musical Revue!*	Musical Revue*
Broadway Heroes	A Closer Walk with Patsy Cline	Shear Madness
Les Feux Follets	Les Feux Follets	Celtic Blaze
Fete Acadienne*	Hedgerow	Les Feux Follets
The Music of Acadie	C'est What?	Confederation Bridge Summer
The Cottars	Confederation Bridge Summer	Concert Series
Island Flavours*	Concert Series	

2007	2008
Anne of Green Gables*	Anne of Green Gables*
British Invation	America Strikes Back
Shear Madness	Stones in his Pocket
Satl Water Moon	
Alberta Fusion	
Confederation Bridge Summer Concert Series	
Toby Tarnow: Children's Plays*	

NOTE: * indicates productions by the Festival / production originale du Festival

Index